HERE WE ARE

HERE WE ARE

FEMINISM
FOR THE REAL WORLD

EDITED BY KELLY JENSEN

Algonquin 2017

Published by Algonquin Young Readers
an imprint of Algonquin Books of Chapel Hill
Post Office Box 2225
Chapel Hill, North Carolina 27515-2225

a division of Workman Publishing
225 Varick Street
New York, New York 10014

Printed in the United States of America.
Published simultaneously in Canada by
Thomas Allen & Son Limited.

Book design, hand-lettering, collage and illustrations
(unless otherwise noted) by Laura Palese.

Grateful acknowledgment is made to the holders of copyright,
publishers, or representatives on pages 227–228, which
constitute an extension of the copyright page.

LIBRARY OF CONGRESS CATALOGING-IN-PUBLICATION DATA
Names: Jensen, Kelly, editor.
Title: Here we are : feminism for the real world / edited by Kelly Jensen.
Other titles: Feminism for the real world
Description: First edition. | Chapel Hill, North Carolina : Algonquin
Young Readers, 2017. | Audience: Ages 14 & up. | Audience: Grades 9 & up. |
"Published simultaneously in Canada by Thomas Allen & Son Limited."
Identifiers: LCCN 2016032054 | ISBN 9781616205867
Subjects: LCSH: Feminism—Juvenile literature. | Feminists—Juvenile
literature. | Women—Social conditions—Juvenile literature. | CYAC:
Feminism. | Feminists. | Women—Social conditions.
Classification: LCC HQ1154 .H468 2017 | DDC 305.42—dc23
LC record available at https://lccn.loc.gov/2016032054

10 9 8 7 6 5 4 3 2 1
First Edition

FOR THOSE WHO *Started* the JOURNEY *and* FOR THOSE WHO WILL CONTINUE IT

CONTENTS

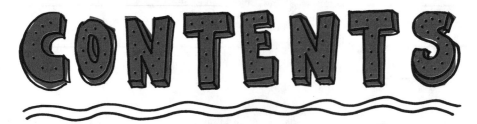

CHAPTER 7
GO YOUR OWN WAY 184

Join the FEMINIST PARTY:

AN INTRODUCTION

Here We Are: Feminism for the Real World
is a guide to understanding what it means
to be a feminist and an invitation to one
of the most important, life-changing,
and exciting parties around.

This is a chance to dive in and out of the different experiences, ideas, and beliefs that underlie feminism.

Feminists come in every shape, size, form, and background. What unites feminists is the belief that every person—regardless of gender, class, education, race, sexuality, or ability—deserves equality. This is a movement about embracing differences and encouraging change that benefits all facets of society. This is a movement about listening as much as it is about speaking up.

Here We Are: Feminism for the Real World aims to enlighten, inspire, and encourage critical thinking, as well as thoughtful action in your every-day life.

LET'S GET THE FEMINIST PARTY STARTED!

CHAPTER one

Starting the JOURNEY

THE PEOPLE
<--- AND THE ---->
W🌍RLD
around us

shape our individual paths
to feminism.

There's no right way and no wrong way. There are no dead ends. The journey is always changing, always shifting, and influenced by our own experiences and perspectives.

Whether you identify as a feminist now or are curious about how people come to label themselves as feminists and own that identity, these pieces will help as you begin your journey through the various paths, influences, and experiences toward feminism.

Forever Feminist

BY MALINDA LO

Fifteen years after high school, I'm in an old friend's apartment, where he has pulled out the yearbook from our senior year. He flips eagerly to a page at the back, in the section of the yearbook dedicated to parting notes. There's my message to him, and, at the bottom, where I signed off, a valediction I don't remember writing: "Forever feminist."

It makes me laugh—uncomfortably, because instantly I am once again an awkward, outspoken girl in glasses with a stereotypical Asian bob haircut, pretending to fit in though I'm desperate to leave my small town behind. But even as my past self flashes into sharp relief, I feel as if I'm gazing at a missive from another world. The passage of time erases so much. What did I mean by that valediction? Why did I write it? Who was I back then?

High school yearbooks are littered with exhortations to "Stay the same!" or "Don't change!" They are futile protests against the inevitable transition from adolescence into adulthood. Maybe the "forever" in my valediction was a similar attempt to declare my unwavering selfhood even though I sensed change coming like a spring flood down a mountainside. Already, I could hear the muted roar in the distance.

But what did I mean by "feminist"? In order to understand this message from the past, I have to excavate my own memory, dig through layer upon layer of accreted experience to expose the girl I once was, the girl I grew out of and away from. Who was she? And am I still that girl?

My personal ideal of a "feminist" is rooted in one woman: my paternal grandmother, Ruth Earnshaw Lo. She was a white American woman who fell in love with a Chinese man at the University of Chicago in the 1930s, where she was an undergraduate and he was a graduate student. When they met, interracial marriage was still not legal nationwide in the United States; Loving v. Virginia did not declare an end to anti-miscegenation laws until 1967. So, in 1937, my grandmother married my grandfather, John Chuanfang Lo, in Shanghai. The day after their wedding, the Japanese invaded Shanghai, sending my grandparents fleeing down the Yangtze River and ultimately all the way to Yunnan Province on the border of Burma, where they were refugees during World War II.

I grew up on stories about my family's life and hardships in China, and many of those stories were told to me by my grandmother, beginning when I was very young. If those stories were dotted with tragedies, they were also leavened with sharp humor and a make-do, survivor mentality. My grandmother told stories about her time "refugeeing" in Yunnan, rationing out the last of their coffee, learning how to bake Western bread and pies with limited Chinese ingredients. She told stories about an American pilot—a Flying Tiger—who crashed near her home and was astonished to encounter an American woman in the middle of nowhere, Asia. She told stories about flying in a U.S. cargo plane over the Hump of the Himalayas into India, with an oxygen mask on her face and a parachute strapped to her back in case the plane was shot down. That flight was only step one of a months-long journey, mostly by sea, from India to Australia to South America to Los Angeles, where en route she discovered she was pregnant with my father.

The rest of my grandmother's life was equally dramatic. She and my grandfather returned to China in 1947, hoping to help rebuild his homeland after the devastation of war, and they stayed after the Communists took over in 1949. It seems naive in retrospect, but back then, nobody knew how repressive Mao Zedong's regime would be. My grandmother ended up spending the next thirty years in China, unable to leave until 1978, after Mao's death opened the door once again to the West. My grandmother wrote a memoir about her experiences titled *In the Eye of the Typhoon*, and it was published in 1980, when I was six years old. I grew up knowing two things for sure: my grandmother was a writer, and I wanted to be like her.

My grandmother was a woman who had the courage to go after what she wanted. She had the hard-won savvy of someone who had lived through countless tumultuous experiences and come out the other side not only whole, but somehow improved. She cultivated an air of mystery and a biting wit, and she always encouraged me to write. Some of my earliest memories are of inventing stories with her, and as I grew up and began to write them down, I shared them with her. She read them with a welcoming seriousness. Without her, I never would have become a writer.

I don't remember talking about feminism with her, and I don't know whether she identified as one, but in my mind, my grandmother was every inch a feminist. It was she who introduced me to many of my other feminist heroes: Louisa May Alcott and her *Little Women*, Madeleine L'Engle and her wonderful novels, the poet Edna St. Vincent Millay.

When I was growing up, I took refuge in fiction and poetry because the real world made me feel like a perpetual outsider. I was one of four Asian American students in my small town; I can remember each of their names and faces even today. It was always clear to me that I was not like everyone else, and though my grandmother's stories made me proud of my family's background, I yearned to be accepted like any other American kid—to be normal. Between the pages of a book, the heroines I loved most weren't Asian, but they did not judge me for being different. When I was in their worlds, I *was* normal. After reading *Anne of Green Gables*, I talked to my grandmother about it, and she told me, "Well, you *are* Anne."

For many girls, their favorite character in *Little Women* is the high-spirited, tomboyish Jo March. When I began to read the novel, I, too, was immediately sympathetic to the adventurous Jo. I was the opposite of a tomboy, but like Jo, I also wanted to be a writer, and I identified with her struggles. I was so thoroughly invested in Jo and her dreams of literary success that when she cast them aside to marry Professor Bhaer and open a school for boys, I felt personally betrayed by her. At the same time, I had developed a growing appreciation for the most popularly reviled sister, Amy. From an early age, Amy wanted to be an artist, but unlike Jo—who seemed, to me, to give up—Amy ultimately became the artist she dreamed of being. For many readers, Amy was selfish and spoiled, but I saw her as someone who knew what she wanted and had the courage to go after it. I might have been Anne Shirley, but I was also Amy March—determined, prickly, and unapologetic.

I also identified strongly with Vicky Austin, the main character in several of Madeleine L'Engle's Austin Family novels, including my favorite, *A Ring of Endless Light*. Unlike L'Engle's better-known Murry Family series (a.k.a. the Time Quintet), the Austin Family series was rooted in low-key if idealized normalcy. I sometimes wished I were part of a family like theirs, because they fit in wherever they went; they were unquestionably American. Vicky wasn't a math geek like Meg Murry; she was a bookish girl who wrote poetry, like me. She was quiet, caring, and generally sensible, but she was never a Goody Two-shoes. Her sensible side could be swayed by the boys she fell for, even if she suspected she was making bad choices. She was imperfect and human and real: I was her, too.

I was fifteen years old when my grandmother gave me a book of Edna St. Vincent Millay's collected poems, and the poet's words lit me up inside. "My candle burns at both ends," she wrote in a joyful declaration sure to find sympathy in any teenager. She was passionate and also precise about her passion. Her words were bracing and beautiful, and they showed me hints of an adult world I knew little about but longed to be part of. I would not know until years later how transgressive Millay was, both as a feminist and an openly bisexual woman, but my grandmother—whose youth was spent in the United States during Millay's heyday in the 1920s—undoubtedly knew. I like to think that my grandmother offered Millay's poems to me as a charge: to be bold, to speak my mind, to embrace my passions.

None of my literary heroines spoke overtly about feminism—at least not that I was aware of at the time. But in Anne Shirley and Amy March, in Vicky Austin and Edna St. Vincent Millay, I saw all the ideals of feminism. Self-motivated, not selfish. Human, not perfect. Bold and adventurous in spirit—just like my grandmother.

In high school, I was like a bottle of soda pop shaken up but unopened, all tightly suppressed bubbles waiting to explode in every direction. I yearned to be normal, but I didn't believe I ever could be. I didn't know much about the complexities of feminism or the academic or political arguments about what it meant, but at a gut level, I got it. I was a feminist, even if it was my own definition, derived from novels and poetry and my grandmother.

When I was seventeen, to me a feminist was someone who lived life fully, who endured what came at her and triumphed over it. A feminist was someone who acted, who set her sights on a dream and made it come true. A feminist was someone who loved deeply, and who allowed that love to change her. She was complicated and sometimes contradictory, witty and full of integrity. A feminist, in my mind, was a woman at full potential.

I am not the same person I was when I was seventeen, but she is still a part of me. I moved away from Colorado and found people like me at college and in the cities I've lived in, but I still go home every year. I have become much more comfortable with my Asian Americanness, but I have also become much more aware of how it sets me apart. I married a woman rather than a man, but I still remember the genuine attraction I had to boys, both fictional and real. I am still inspired by my grandmother, and I miss her every day.

I know now that "feminist" is a charged and contested concept. It is not meant only for women; it is also meant for men, and it challenges the deeply held belief that gender is a binary system, with women on one side and men on the other. Feminism is about recognizing power and fighting to distribute it equally, regardless of race or class or ability or gender. Feminism is not static, and it never has been. In fact, feminism demands change.

I'd like to see my high school yearbook valediction of "forever feminist" as a commitment to this change, a "forever" commitment to making the world a more equal place. Or, maybe I wrote "forever feminist" as a goal for myself, a declaration that I would never stop trying to live my life at full potential. If so, it's a goal I intend to reach.

What Does "Feminism" Mean? A Brief History of the Word, from Its Beginnings All the Way up to the Present

BY SUZANNAH WEISS

Amid recent efforts to get people to stop shying away from the label "feminist" and the debate over what "feminism" means and who gets to decide on a definition, I decided to do some digging into the history of the word "feminism." What I've found might surprise you, make you laugh, and possibly depress you a little. That said, I hereby present to you a brief, non-comprehensive history of the use of the word "feminism."[1]

THE FIRST WAVE, PART I: THE NINETEENTH CENTURY

According to the *New World Encyclopedia*, the term's earliest roots are connected to two things with which feminists are often associated, whether rightly or wrongfully: France and socialism. In fact, its French translation, *féminisme*, was first used by French socialist Charles Fourier[2] in 1837 to describe the emancipation of women he envisioned for his utopian future. The first documented English use appears in Volume 13 of *De Bow's Review of the Southern and Western States*, a business magazine from the American South, in 1852:

The reforming ladies have not yet got an "ism" for their move; but have nevertheless come forward scarcely less boldly than their masculine co-adjutors . . . Our attention has happened to fall upon Mrs. E. O. Smith, who is, we are informed, among the most moderate of the feminist re-formers! Tolerably fair specimens of the other extreme have been made public in the sundry women-convention reports which have appeared . . .

THE FIRST WAVE, PART II: THE EARLY TWENTIETH CENTURY

The *Oxford English Dictionary* confirms that "feminist" first appeared there in the late 1800s. But in 1914, there was still some confusion over the term, as Bucky Turco documents.[3] An article from that year in the North Carolina newspaper the *Robesonian* sums up a misconception many are still working through today: "We are asked, what is feminism? We supposed it is a new term to describe the womanly woman as distinguished from effemi-nacy. It is rather a term that embodies woman's [sic] rights." Go figure.

The *New York Times* published a more evolved characterization of feminism by women's suffrage activist Carrie Chapman Catt that same year:

> WHAT is feminism? A world-wide revolt against all artificial barriers which laws and customs interpose betwen [sic] women and human freedom. It is born of the instinct within every natural woman's soul that God designed her as the equal, the co-worker, the comrade of the men of her family, and not as their slave, or servant, or dependent, or plaything.[4]

A century ago, in 1915, the *Washington Herald* interviewed several people about feminism but said most of the responses were not in plain English. Their favorite one, though, was: "Feminism is the doctrine of the social, legal, and political equality of the sexes."[5] Hey, that's not too different from the modern definition![6]

However, English actress and suffragist Beatrice Forbes-Robertson Hale gave a very different explanation in 1917, according to Pennsylvania newspaper the *Reading Eagle*: "The three cardinal principles in the movement are: [t]he development of the highest type of monogamy; the recognition of the single standard of morals and the consecration of the best thought of parents to the interests of their children." To me, that just sounds like morality, yet it was delivered in a lecture to the Brooklyn Ethical Culture Society titled "What Is Feminism?"

That same year, a *Sydney Morning Herald* review of W. L. George's *The Intelligence of Woman* quoted a passage from the book that is surprisingly reflective of modern gender politics: "There are no men and there are no women; there are only sexual majorities." According to the review, which spends more time criticizing George's writing style than addressing her points, George believes a feminist is more radical than a suffragist, wanting to not just attain equal rights for women but also challenge what it means to be a woman or a man.

THE SECOND WAVE: 1950 TO 1990

Voting rights were indeed a focus of first-wave feminism, but second-wave feminism (technically from the 1960s through the 1980s, with a little spillover on either side) brought gender itself to the forefront, though historians still say the largest issues it addressed were sexuality and reproductive rights. The 1949 publication of Simone de Beauvoir's *The Second Sex*[7] in France (followed by a 1953 publication in the United States) is sometimes considered the inaugural event of second-wave feminism. Drawing from existential philosophy, Beauvoir's "founding text of feminism"[8] famously states that "one is not born, but rather becomes, a woman"—a claim that has left even many of today's pundits aghast. Yet Beauvoir initially dissociated herself from women's movements[9] because she believed economic reform was the solution to gender inequality. In 1972, however, she stated in an interview with Alice Schwarzer that she'd reached the conclusion that she was in fact a feminist.

During feminism's second wave, a few notable definitions emerged, including writer Marie Shear's sarcastic remark that "feminism is the radical notion that women are people"[10] and this eloquent explanation from Adrienne Rich: "Feminism means finally that we renounce our obedience to the fathers and recognize that the world they have described is not the whole world . . . Feminism implies that we recognize fully the inadequacy for us, the distortion, of male-created ideologies, and that we proceed to think, and act, out of that recognition."[11]

THE THIRD WAVE: 1990 AND BEYOND

Fast-forward to the 1990s, when third-wave feminism brought the dismantling of gender and other categories to front and center. Third-wave feminism, which we're now experiencing (though some scholars have said we're entering a fourth wave),[12] is focused on challenging the gender binary and making room for the LGBT community and other diverse perspectives within feminism. During this time, feminism has become a popular topic of discussion, with the use of the word "feminism" in books peaking in 1995.

As feminism has gained widespread publicity, however, it has also accrued backlash. Members of the Women Against Feminism[13] movement started sharing photos of themselves holding signs describing why they don't need feminism in 2014. Many celebrities also have recently spoken against feminism,[14] saying it's "too strong" or "alienating," though a notable number have also voiced their support.[15]

In 2014, *Time* included "feminist" in a poll asking readers which words we should ban in 2015,[16] suggesting that the trend of celebrities from Miley Cyrus[17] to Taylor Swift[18] announcing their feminist status trivialized the movement. After receiving backlash for reinforcing the popular notion that "feminist" is a word to avoid, *Time* apologized for including it in the poll.

But pressure to abolish the word "feminism" lives on. If I Google "feminism is," "for everybody" pops up first, but this is directly followed by "bullshit," "cancer," and "bad."

In addition, the #WomenAgainstFeminism hashtag is alive and well on Twitter, with women arguing that feminism actually impedes gender equality.

The definition and value of feminism seem to be as much under debate as they were a century ago, so who knows how much longer we'll be fighting this battle to win feminism mainstream acceptance. But here's to hoping the coming years will see more victories in favor of feminism, both the word and the movement.

THIS PIECE WAS PREVIOUSLY PUBLISHED ON BUSTLE.COM.

1 http://ratter.com/ratter/all/heyday-in-tabloids/213973-what-is-feminism.
2 http://www.newworldencyclopedia.org/entry/Charles_Fourier.
3 http://ratter.com/ratter/all/heyday-in-tabloids/213973-what-is-feminism.
4 "'Free Love' Charge Held Ridiculous," Carrie Chapman Catt, *New York Times*, February 15, 1914.
5 http://ratter.com/ratter/all/heyday-in-tabloids/213973-what-is-feminism.
6 http://www.bustle.com/articles/74718-are-you-a-feminist-take-this-quiz-to-find-out-once-and-for-all.
7 http://www.pacificu.edu/about-us/news-events/four-waves-feminism.
8 http://www.nytimes.com/2010/05/30/books/review/Gray-t.html?pagewanted=all&_r=1.
9 http://womenshistory.about.com/od/simonedebeauvoir/a/simone-de-beauvoir-second-wave.htm.
10 http://www.beverlymcphail.com/feminismradicalnotion.html.
11 http://web.stanford.edu/class/fs101/quotes.html.
12 http://www.pacificu.edu/about-us/news-events/four-waves-feminism.
13 http://www.buzzfeed.com/rossalynwarren/i-do-not-think-it-means-what-you-think-it-means #.fjxWGe9J73.
14 http://www.huffingtonpost.com/2013/12/17/feminist-celebrities_n_4460416.html.
15 http://www.bustle.com/articles/102888-11-celebs-who-have-defended-feminism-with-powerful-words.
16 http://time.com/3576870/worst-words-poll-2014/.
17 http://www.huffingtonpost.com/2013/11/14/miley-cyrus-feminist_n_4274194.html.
18 http://www.huffingtonpost.com/2014/08/24/taylor-swift-feminist-_n_5704691.html.

FEMINIST SONGS TO SING ALONG TO

by Kody Keplinger

So you can sing along with your besties, I wanted to put together a playlist of feminist songs with themes ranging from self-acceptance to self-love, from female friendships to teaming up against the patriarchy. Consider this my mixtape for you.

"Can't Hold Us Down" by Christina Aguilera & Lil' Kim

"Dancing with Myself" by the Donnas

"Flawless" by Beyoncé

"Follow Your Arrow" by Kacey Musgraves

"Girlfriend" by Icona Pop

"Love Myself" by Hailee Steinfeld

"One Girl Revolution" by Superchick

"Proud" by Tegan & Sara

"Rebel Girl" by Bikini Kill

"Salute" by Little Mix

"The Schuyler Sisters" by the Hamilton Broadway Cast

"Secrets" by Mary Lambert

"Video" by India.Arie

Bad Feminist: Take Two

BY ROXANE GAY

I am failing as a woman. I am failing as a feminist. To freely accept the feminist label would not be fair to good feminists. If I am, indeed, a feminist, I am a rather bad one. I am a mess of contradictions. There are many ways in which I am doing feminism wrong, at least according to the way my perceptions of feminism have been warped by being a woman.

I want to be independent, but I want to be taken care of and have someone to come home to. I have a job I'm pretty good at. I am in charge of things. I am on committees. People respect me and take my counsel. I want to be strong and professional, but I resent how hard I have to work to be taken seriously, to receive a fraction of the consideration I might otherwise receive. Sometimes I feel an overwhelming need to cry at work, so I close my office door and lose it.

I want to be in charge, respected, in control, but I want to surrender, completely, in certain aspects of my life. Who wants to grow up?

When I drive to work, I listen to thuggish rap at a very loud volume, even though the lyrics are degrading to women and offend me to my core. The classic Ying Yang Twins song "Salt Shaker"? It's amazing. "Bitch you gotta shake it till your camel starts to hurt."
Poetry.

(I am mortified by my music choices.)

I care what people think.

Pink is my favorite color. I used to say my favorite color was black to be cool, but it is pink—all shades of pink. If I have an accessory, it is probably pink. I read *Vogue*, and I'm not doing it ironically. I once live-tweeted the

September issue. I love dresses. For years I pretended I hated them, but I don't. Maxi dresses are one of the finest clothing items to become popular in recent memory. I have opinions on maxi dresses! I shave my legs! Again, this mortifies me. If I take issue with the unrealistic standards of beauty women are held to, I shouldn't have a secret fondness for fashion and smooth calves, right?

I know nothing about cars. When I take my car to the mechanic, they are speaking a foreign language. A mechanic asks what's wrong with my car, and I stutter things like, "Well, there's a sound I try to drown out with my radio." The windshield-wiper fluid for the rear window of my car no longer sprays the window. It just sprays the air. I don't know how to deal with this. It feels like an expensive problem. I still call my father with questions about cars and am not terribly interested in changing any of my car-related ignorance. I don't want to be good at cars. Good feminists, I assume, are independent enough to address vehicular crises on their own; they are independent enough to care.

Despite what people think based on my writing, I very much like men. They're interesting to me, and I mostly wish they'd be better about how they treat women so I wouldn't have to call them out so often. And still, I put up with nonsense from unsuitable men even though I know better and can do better. I love diamonds and the excess of weddings. I consider certain domestic tasks as gendered, mostly all in my favor because I don't care for chores—lawn care, bug killing, and trash removal, for example, are men's work.

Sometimes—a lot of the time, honestly—I totally fake "it" because it's easier. I am a fan of orgasms, but they take time, and in many instances I don't want to spend that time. All too often I don't really like the guy enough to explain the calculus of my desire. Then I feel guilty because the sisterhood would not approve. I'm not even sure what the sisterhood is, but the idea of a sisterhood menaces me, quietly, reminding me of how bad a feminist I am. Good feminists don't fear the sisterhood because they know they are comporting themselves in sisterhood-approved ways.

I love babies, and I want to have one. I am willing to make certain compromises (not sacrifices) in order to do so—namely, maternity leave and slowing down at work to spend more time with my child, writing less, so I can be more present in my life. I worry about dying alone, unmarried and childless, because I spent so much time pursuing my career and accumulating degrees. This kind of thinking keeps me up at night, but I pretend it doesn't because I am supposed to be evolved. My success, such as it is, is supposed to be enough if I'm a good feminist. It is not enough. It is not even close.

Because I have so many deeply held opinions about gender equality, I feel a lot of pressure to live up to certain ideals. I am supposed to be a good feminist who is having it all, doing it all. Really, though, I'm a woman in her thirties, struggling to accept herself and her credit score. For so long I told myself I was not this woman—utterly human and flawed. I worked overtime to be anything but this woman, and it was exhausting and unsustainable and even harder than simply embracing who I am.

Maybe I'm a bad feminist, but I am deeply committed to the issues important to the feminist movement. I have strong opinions about misogyny, institutional sexism that consistently places women at a disadvantage, the inequity in pay, the cult of beauty and thinness, the repeated attacks on reproductive freedom, violence against women, and on and on. I am as committed to fighting fiercely for equality as I am committed to disrupting the notion that there is an essential feminism.

I am the kind of feminist who is appalled by the phrase "legitimate rape" and by political candidates such as Missouri's Todd Akin, who in an interview reaffirmed his commitment to opposing abortion, almost unilaterally. He said, "If it's a legitimate rape, the female body has ways to shut that whole thing down. But let's assume that maybe that didn't work or something: I think there should be some punishment, but the punishment ought to be of the rapist, and not attacking the child," drawing from pseudoscience and a lax cultural attitude toward rape.

Being feminist, however, even a bad one, has also taught me that the need for feminism and advocacy also applies to seemingly less serious issues like a Top 40 song or a comedian's puerile humor. The existence of these lesser artifacts of our popular culture is made possible by the far graver issues we are facing. The ground has long been softened.

At some point, I got it into my head that a feminist was a certain kind of woman. I bought into grossly inaccurate myths about who feminists are—militant, perfect in their politics and person, man-hating, humorless. I bought into these myths even though, intellectually, I *know* better. I'm not proud of this. I don't want to buy into these myths anymore. I don't want to cavalierly disavow feminism like far too many other women have done.

Bad feminism seems the only way I can both embrace myself as a feminist and be myself, so I write. I chatter away on Twitter about everything that makes me angry and all the small things that bring me joy. I write blogposts about the meals I cook as I try to take better care of myself, and with each new entry I realize that I'm "undestroying" myself after years of allowing myself to stay damaged. The more I write, the more I put myself out into the world as a bad feminist but, I hope, a good woman—I am being open about who I am and who I was and where I have faltered and who I would like to become.

No matter what issues I have with feminism, I am a feminist. I cannot and will not deny the importance and absolute necessity of feminism. Like most people, I'm full of contradictions, but I also don't want to be treated like shit for being a woman.

I am a bad feminist. I would rather be a bad feminist than no feminist at all.

THIS PIECE WAS PREVIOUSLY PUBLISHED IN *BAD FEMINIST: ESSAYS* BY ROXANE GAY.

FAQs ABOUT FEMINISM

Can men be feminists?

Anyone, no matter what gender identity they do or don't decide to take, can be a feminist. All that's required to be feminist is the belief that everyone deserves equal opportunities.

What does intersectional feminism mean?

Kimberlé Crenshaw coined the term "intersectional feminism" in 1989. The idea is that all forms of oppression intersect and should be considered at those intersections. In other words, a black woman not only has the social challenge of being female; she also faces the social challenges of being black. The intersection of her race and her gender matters. Challenges for a black woman may mirror many that a white woman may face, but the addition of the black woman's race compounds the challenges of her social status.

The essays in this collection highlight intersectionality ranging from disability and feminism to race and feminism to gender and feminism, and more. To be an intersectional feminist, one must acknowledge that there are layers of complexity in each individual's life.

Privilege

BY MATT NATHANSON

I am a straight white man. My voice dominates.

This country was built around voices like mine, privileged voices. To speak out on the topic of gay/queer/transgender rights, to speak out on the topic of black lives mattering . . . I have learned that having my voice heard, even if I am on the side of the oppressed, is not important. In fact, it can be a detriment.

Everyone has heard enough from voices like mine. My actions, my clearing of space for the voices of those oppressed, *that* is my job. That is where I can best be of service. To make room in my privilege for the voices of others to be heard.

It is in listening to other voices that I have learned. It is in experiencing the stories of others that I have grown.

I am best served being awake. Being quiet. And paying attention.

So when I was asked to write this essay on feminism, not only did I feel unqualified; I felt irrelevant. Feminism? I'm not sure I even know what that word really means. I understand the definition, but I've never had to know it in my bones.

As a man, if I go for a job, I will make more than a woman with the same qualifications. When I walk down a street alone at night, or take a cab by myself, I have never feared being raped. I am not catcalled or called a "bitch" because I don't return a look. I do not have entire industries built around making millions of dollars telling me what my "beautiful" is. I do not have a battalion of old men putting laws in place, telling me what I can and can't do with my body.

Feminism is not about me, right?

I am awake on this issue, but I am far from perfect. I still engage in the sexist patterns of the "un-awoke" me, and even though I'm more vigilant about rooting them out now, and disassembling them, those patterns creep in. Like describing Ann Wilson, from the band Heart, as my favorite female singer, but describing Bono, from the band U2, as my favorite singer. Or responding with a "no" when someone asks me if my wife is currently working, instead of taking the time to explain that she is a stay-at-home mother, and that is a *very* real job. No less real than mine. The list goes on.

And on a very selfish level, I don't want to hear from people who disagree with me. "Feminism" can be a hand grenade of a topic. Writing about feminism invites people who feel threatened by it to rain down their opinion. And I don't want to hear that kind of ignorance. It depresses me. I don't want to hear the people who are standing still, yelling at progress and change and equality.

At forty-two years old, I try to live my life without that kind of negative energy. I have softened into the position that my job is not to educate those who don't want to learn. But there it is again . . . my privilege, rearing its ugly head. I don't need to take this topic of feminism on because it does not directly affect me. I can opt out.

But can I really? Do I want to build my life on the foundation of my straight white male privilege? No, I don't.

I have a daughter. She's five, and I am in awe of her greatness. Her comic timing, her powerful body, her brain and the way it processes the world. The way she expresses herself without limits. She's naked all the time, and she never questions her body. She loves it. She doesn't judge herself against kids with different body types, or actresses on television or photoshopped ads in magazines.

One minute, she talks about being an astronaut; the next, she talks about being a singer. Then a veterinarian. Then the president of the United States. And a mother. She has not yet taken "no" for an answer from the world. But I know she is entering into this world. Adolescence and adulthood will try to steal that "wide-openness" from her, and the world will tell her she can't do everything.

Over and over, because she is a woman, the world will close doors that should be open to all. And she will have to work ten times as hard to get through them.

When I watch TV, I notice how insidiously pro-male the message is.

Women are support.

Women are accessories.

Women wait to be saved.

Women play the assistant, not the magician.

Women need men to be complete.

My daughter is going to hit this stuff head-on, and my wife and I are not always going to be there to help her course-correct. How is she going to handle her own sexuality? And how is she going to handle *other* people and her own sexuality? That just feels like a minefield, a place where the world is gonna do its best to knock her off course. She is tall and she is substantially built. At what point are we going to have to reassure her that her body is beautiful? How many times will we have to remind her that her vulva and vagina are her own, that her breasts and her body are her own? That they are hers and hers alone to make mistakes with, to connect with, to have beautiful experiences with, to share with whomever she chooses?

And society will want to vilify her for *loving* herself and for the choices she will make in pursuit of that love.

Isn't it wild the way our puritanical culture represses women's love of their own bodies, their discovery and the joy of their sexual experiences? All the things that my kid should be able to naturally be, she is going to have to defend. She is going to have to become skilled at dismantling the information that comes in, sifting through the noise and the human collision, and *not* allowing it to reshape her in the image of the distorted sexist lens of our culture.

My daughter has a set of hurdles in place that I never had. She is privileged in her own ways, too—I am not downplaying that—but she is heading out into a game that is fixed. It's rigged against her, and she will have to spend a lot of her energy carving out space for herself among men. Just getting herself on equal footing. And it is my obligation as a parent to help her.

But feminism—and I am talking about intersectional feminism here—is more than that. And saying that my involvement in feminism is for my daughter is, again, part of the problem.

As an awake man, I need to acknowledge that feminism benefits me. Feminism seeks to dismantle *all* gender stereotypes. By redefining what it means to be a "woman," feminism also redefines what it means to be a "man." And to live in a world where men are encouraged to express their full range of emotions, where they are encouraged to be their own unique selves without being anchored down to some narrow, societal definition of "masculinity"? *Count. Me. In.*

I want to live in a world of freedom and acceptance. A place that makes space for *everyone* to feel comfortable. Where there are no dark places to hide. No ridicule.

Am I being idealistic? Of course . . . but is there really any other way to be?

We need to evolve. We do not need a system that creates any more repressed, ashamed humans, male, female or nonbinary. Dismantling this system, this fear, is revolutionary, and feminism has always been a crucial building block of this revolution.

And the change that it will bring will benefit us all.

I make space in my life for feminism. I include it in my values. I stay awake on this issue and process it out loud here, with you.

For my daughter.

For myself.

For the world I live in.

And for the world I want.

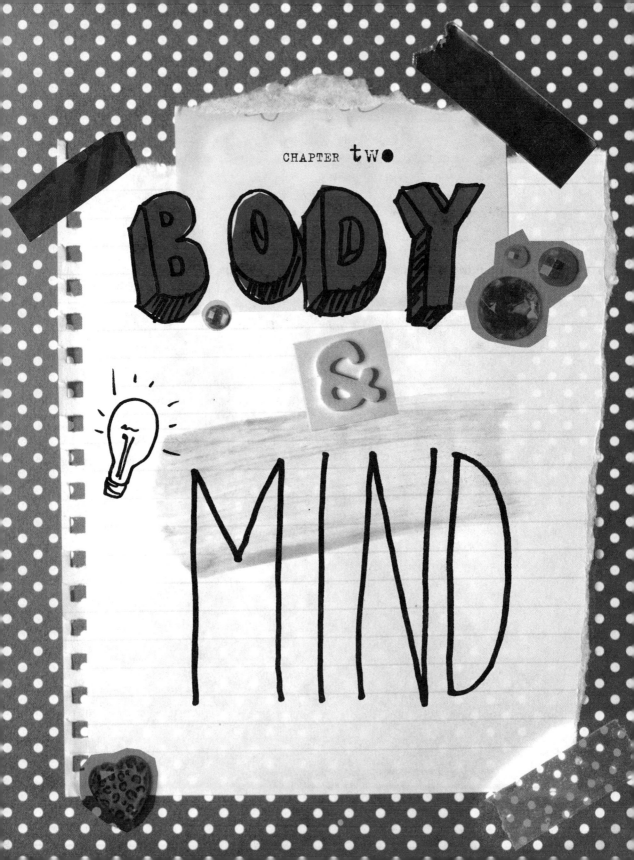

CHAPTER two

BODY & MIND

Here's the TRUTH about

FEMINISTS:

THEY COME IN ALL SHAPES SIZES AND COLORS.

Feminism is not a physical

UNIFORM.

Sometimes feminists wear makeup and sometimes they don't. Sometimes they wear dresses; sometimes they don't. Sometimes they shave their legs and other times, they choose not to. Sometimes they perform the female identity and sometimes they perform the male identity; still other times, feminists choose not to identify as any particular gender at all.

Feminism isn't about the specific, individual choices people make in how they look and feel. Feminism is about an individual's ability to make choices about how they look and feel and take care of themselves.

These pieces explore the ways the body and the mind do—and sometimes don't—work. They take a magnifying glass to the assumptions of what it means to be and live in one's body and mind and how those things relate to feminism.

The Monster Book of Questions and Answers

BY ANNE THÉRIAULT

Mental illness and adolescence have always been deeply intertwined for me, to the point where I can't really consider one without thinking of the other. I suspect this is true for a lot of people. The two conditions feed into each other and off each other; hormones flood neural pathways, and drowned networks scramble to recalibrate their settings. Your world shifts—sometimes slowly, sometimes with a jarring suddenness—and you struggle to shift with it. Things that seemed clear before now look like they're reflected in a funhouse mirror. Nothing is what you expected; nothing feels solid.

And if I can't separate my experience of mental illness from my experience of life as a teenager, the same holds true for how I view feminism and mental health. Women have been called different variations of crazy since the beginning of recorded history, with labels like "hysterical" being used to silence them, discredit them, and invalidate their opinions. These ideas persist even today—I know I've definitely heard my fair share of "crazy ex-girlfriend" stories, most of which boil down to "the girl I dated had too many feelings" or "my ex wouldn't let me do whatever I wanted." So part of my feminism means breaking down stereotypes like this that are generally harmful to women.

In a broader sense, feminism should also be engaged with mental health activism because people who live with mental illness face stigma and discrimination. For example, you can't call in sick with a bad case of the sads, so even if you're feeling too depressed or anxious to leave the house, you have to either tough it out or fake a convincing cough when you're on the phone with your boss. Schools and workplaces often lack accommodation for people with mental illness, which means that it can be hard to get good grades or keep a steady job. And, of course, mental illness itself is the punchline to so many hurtful jokes—if you don't think it's okay to laugh at someone with a physical illness or disability, why is it funny if someone is mentally ill? Feminism should be about breaking down all kinds of different power structures, and the harmful way our culture views mental illness should be one of them.

I found the lump just a few days after my eleventh birthday. It was a soft little swollen spot next to one of my nipples, and it hurt when I touched it. I tried poking it lightly; it still hurt. I pressed it harder, thinking that it might be some sort of very deep pimple I could pop. But instead of bursting, the lump slid out from under my fingers. It was a strange little lump that almost seemed to have a life of its own.

I told myself that maybe it was a bruise. I told myself that the lump would be gone by morning. I told myself sternly to go to sleep, but instead I made a ring of stuffed animals on my bed and sat in the middle of it until dawn.

I'd seen enough made-for-TV movies to know that I definitely had cancer. Somewhere deep inside of me, some dark, secret rot had been spreading for weeks, maybe even months. The doctors would have to cut off my breasts before they'd even had the chance to grow. I would have to spend months in the hospital while they dripped poison into my veins and my hair fell out in clumps. My classmates would send me cards and then forget about me, or else visit and linger for a few awkward moments before drifting back out of my room and into their regular kid lives. I imagined the very end, my parents holding my thin white hands as I struggled and then finally failed to breathe.

I decided not to tell anyone about the lump. That way, I figured, I could avoid the hospital and my friends' pity and my parents' grief. Eventually I would just die quietly in my sleep and no one would be the wiser.

I held out for nearly a week—a week colored by a quiet dread that made my chest feel tight and my skin prickle with fear. I finally gave in to that dread on Friday evening, when my father gave me a book he'd bought for me that day. It was called *The Monster Book of Questions and Answers* and had, as you might imagine from the name, a satisfying size and heft. I sat down on the couch with the book in my lap and ran my fingers across its glossy blue cover, but instead of opening it, I burst into panicked sobs.

"I have cancer, and I'm going to die," I half yelled, half wept.

I told them about the lump, of course. And at some point during the denouement that followed, my mother told me that I wasn't sick—the lump was just healthy, growing breast tissue, and my body was just a healthy, growing body. I was so relieved that I started laughing and couldn't stop.

I wasn't going to die! I was just going to grow up.

The dread didn't go away, though. It stayed with me, sometimes dwindling until it was tiny and far away and I could almost forget about it, and sometimes swelling until it obscured everything else. I could feel it when it came on—my scalp would tingle, and my throat and mouth would seem to swell until I had a hard time eating. I didn't worry about cancer anymore, but other ideas consumed me. Images would sometimes pop into my head, and I wouldn't be able to stop thinking about them. One day I pictured my mother and baby sister being hit by a car, and I felt like a monster for even just imagining it. And once the thought had lodged in my mind, I couldn't get rid of it.

These violent mental images weren't proof of my monsterhood, but they were in fact intrusive thoughts—one of the hallmarks of anxiety disorders. Intrusive thoughts are the kind that start out as a tiny blip but somehow burrow deep into your brain. They wake you at three a.m. and keep you up for the rest of the night. Some of them ripen into full-fledged obsessions that you can't shake, while others turn into endless cycles of worry, the kind where the same chain of thoughts keeps looping in your mind like a record that won't stop skipping.

A few years after the dread and the intrusive thoughts set in, I was diagnosed with clinical depression. My doctor referred me to a therapist, but I refused to go back after he laughed at what I'd written on my intake form (under "mood" I'd scrawled "cynical and jaded," which I thought sounded very intelligent and grown-up). I took a lot of different medications; some of them caused insomnia, others brought on a dragging exhaustion that made me fall asleep during class. All of them made my head feel fuzzy. I started skipping school because I couldn't get out of bed in the morning. I failed classes. I was hospitalized.

Things were pretty dark for a while—several whiles, actually.

At the time, I felt like I was the only person going through all of this, but it turned out that wasn't true. In fact, adolescence and early adulthood are the most common times for the onset of mental illness, and one in five American teenagers will experience some kind of mental disorder. All of this makes total sense when you consider both how messy puberty is and how intense the social and academic pressure of high school and university can be. You're supposed to get good grades, participate in extracurricular activities, have a part-time job, and somehow find time for socializing and sleep. Meanwhile your parents are yelling at you to get off the couch and clean your room, and your frenemy is being a passive-aggressive jerk on Instagram, and you feel like you can't possibly surface from this mess and take a deep breath.

Anyone would feel overwhelmed by all of these things. But sometimes what you feel is more than just run-of-the-mill stress. Or maybe it is run-of-the-mill stress, but you need some help coping with it. Maybe you have a mental illness, or maybe you're just going through a hard time. Maybe it's not you but someone you love who's struggling with mental health.

Whatever the case is, if and when you ever get to a point where you feel like you just can't handle it anymore, here are some things I want you to know:

1. YOU ARE NOT ALONE. Even when it absolutely does not feel like it, you have a whole team of people on your side. While this doesn't mean that everyone will always act in helpful and loving ways toward you, it can help to remember that there is likely a whole host of people out there who think you are the opposite of worthless. You're also not alone in the sense that there are so many other people out there living with mental illness. Many of your classmates, teachers, and family struggle with some of the same things you

do. There are a lot of us out there; we make up nearly a quarter of the population. Welcome to the club—it might not be the one you wanted to join and it probably won't help you get into college, but we do have the best snacks.

2. YOU ARE THE EXPERT ON YOURSELF. Only you know what exactly you're going through. You get to decide what happens to your body, which means that if there is a treatment plan being put into place, you get to have some say over what it looks like and how it's implemented.

3. WHATEVER YOU FEEL IS VALID. This doesn't mean that your emotions represent objective realities—for example, even if you *feel* like your friends all hate you, that doesn't necessarily mean they do. But even if your feelings don't reflect an accurate representation of what's happening, that doesn't mean it's wrong or bad for you to have them. There are no right or wrong feelings. However you feel is exactly that: how you feel.

4. YOU GET TO DECIDE HOW YOU IDENTIFY. If you're dealing with mental health issues but don't consider yourself to be mentally ill, that's cool. If, on the other hand, you feel like mental illness makes up part of who you are, that's cool, too. If you want to self-identify as crazy or mad, that's totally fine. But just as no one else gets to decide what your identity is, you have to extend the same courtesy to others. While you might not be bothered by some terms, other people will be. Everyone's experience is different; be gentle with yourself and everyone else you encounter.

5. TALKING MAKES THINGS EASIER. This is a tough one, because I know that talking about mental health is hard. Trust me, I once spent like five years never talking about mental illness except during the secret late-night phone calls I made to crisis lines after everyone else had gone to bed. Eventually, I got to the point where things were so obviously bad that I couldn't *not* talk about it anymore. And you know what? It was such a relief. People have mostly been incredibly lovely and supportive, and I don't feel like I'm telling lies of omission every day. Plus, if I need to cancel plans

because I'm stuck on my couch listening to sad songs and crying, I can just straight up tell people that and they *get it*. You'll be surprised at how much people get it.

6. ROLE MODELS ARE IMPORTANT. I know this sounds like boring, grown-up advice, but I promise it's not. Finding other people who have felt the way you do is like a magic healing balm. For me, it was Sylvia Plath and her journals. When I'm at my most awful, I dive head-first into them and remember that I'm not the only one who feels this dragging misery. Wherever you are right now, I promise you that someone else has been exactly there.

7. YOU HAVE SURVIVED 100 PERCENT OF YOUR WORST DAYS. You might roll your eyes at that—like duh, of course you've survived them, you're here reading this, aren't you? But I want you to remember this the next time you find yourself knee-deep in a day that feels impossible. The fact that you have lived through every single one of your most awful days is legitimate proof that you can do it again. Statistics are on your side. You got this.

8. TO REPEAT: YOU GOT THIS. But on the days when you don't feel like you've got this, it's okay to ask for help.

I'm definitely a grown-up now—I have a job, I'm married, and I have a kid of my own. But there are still days when I'm right back where that eleven-year-old was, my limbs tense with fear and my heart shuddering in my chest. Sometimes I can't get out of bed in the morning. Sometimes I spend the day sobbing into a pillow. But I also have a good life, and I'm mostly okay.

I wish I could write a letter to my younger self and tell her that she's brave and smart and funny and good. I can't, though, so I'm writing to you, to tell you exactly those things. Maybe you don't need to hear this right now, but tuck it away somewhere. Because maybe someday you will.

And that's exactly the note I want to end this on—that short sentence, as a stand-alone thought to frame all of your future accomplishments: someday you will.

The Big Blue Ocean and My Big Fat Body

BY ANGIE MANFREDI

I'll never forget the first time I stepped out into cold, bright blue water, wearing nothing but my swimsuit.

Perhaps that sounds like a regular day at the beach to you, the kind of experience many people have. For most people I bet it is. But for me—for a fat girl—it was a heady rush. There I was, in the Gulf of Mexico, a light breeze on my neck and water lapping around my sizable thighs, and I wasn't covering myself up with a T-shirt or a long gown. It was just me. In my swimsuit.

Wait—maybe I should back up. Maybe you're stuck on that word—"fat." If you're like many people, you have been taught to avoid that word, to shift your eyes politely away. If you're fat yourself, maybe you winced reading it, feeling a slither of discomfort. If you're not fat, you perhaps felt an urge to reach out, pat my hand, and assure me I'm not fat. This is because you have internalized the endless drum of messages about fat bodies that our culture puts out; it's a very natural response.

We are told, all of us, no matter what our size, that fat bodies are *lesser*, that they are somehow abhorrent and definitely repulsive. You can see this in how rarely we see fat heroes or leads in stories, in how models on runways and the pages of magazines are always thin. Our culture reveres thinness—think about how we talk about the goal of thigh gaps and "fitspiration." Fat bodies are the butt of jokes, the punchline. That's why if I say I am fat, I understand that initial feeling of discomfort you may feel—that urge you may have to reach out and take that word away from me.

But I don't want you to.

You see, I've fought for that word. I've fought myself, my own self-shame. I've fought a society that doesn't want to carry clothes that fit me and never shows me images of people with bodies like mine in the entertainment I buy or the culture I participate in. I fought all that for the right to use "fat" with pride. And feminism helped me take it back.

I *am* fat. I can tell you how much I weigh. I can show you pictures. I can tell you what my dress size is. Though maybe that will change between my writing this and your reading it since none of this is ever static. All of those things are my body, the definition of my very own *self*. But none of these things are either good or bad.

You've probably heard people use other terms to avoid using "fat." I know all the words, too. Some popular choices are curvy, chubby, or fluffy. Those are fine words, and if you choose one to define how *you* think about *your* body, that's great. But for me, none of them fits. Because they just don't describe what my body is. My body is fat. I won't win any awards or lose any points for saying that. I am merely stating a fact: I am fat.

You may have to take many small steps to reach this kind of body confidence. It's hard. I know how hard it is. I also know it's a road we all have to keep walking. You'll have hard days when you just can't continue. You'll hear hateful things and your self-esteem will crash, or you'll have hard days when clothes don't fit right or when you get winded before everyone else. That's okay. That's all okay. You are not alone. You are never alone on this path. Others are walking right beside you, trying their best to accept and love their own bodies. It's hard work, but we are in this together.

Here's a mental exercise that has helped me. When I can't escape hateful, mean thoughts about my body, I ask myself what I would do if I heard someone talking that way about a friend. I would speak up for my friend. I would defend her and boost her up. So if you have a day when you hate yourself and your body, try to think of *yourself* as a friend. Be kind to yourself, defend yourself, be your own friend. Even—especially—when you are confronting hard days.

Maybe you're fat, too. Maybe you're afraid you are. Maybe people tell you that you are, and you can tell that they mean "fat" as an insult, as a thing you should be ashamed of. Maybe people demand justifications from you about why you look the way you do. But you don't owe anyone an explanation of the hows and whys of your body, and you shouldn't be ashamed of your body any more than you should be ashamed of having brown hair or needing glasses. Those aren't good or bad moral judgments about you, either—they just *are*. You have a right to exist just as *you* are. You have value and worth just as you are.

Feminism helped me understand that my body was not up for public debate and discussion. Feminism reminds us that people have inherent worth for who they are, not how they look. The way you look is fleeting. Tomorrow you could cut off all your hair or get burned in a fire. But inside, you would still be *you*. Feminism teaches that you have worth and value; you have something to say worth hearing no matter how you look—no matter how fat you are.

Once I began to connect feminism with body image, I was able to see that my body, my *fat*, wasn't a judgment. It wasn't a decree that I was worth less. Feminism taught me that I could be free of my own hatred and shame, that I could stop trying to find subtler words to refer to only one part of what makes me.

Feminism helped me step out into that cool, bright blue water on a beautiful day as a fat girl in a swimsuit because feminism helped me see that I deserve the same things as everyone else. You, too, have the right to enjoy the big blue ocean on your terms and for *yourself*.

I'd always known that feminism is about freeing us from society's expectations of what girls and women should look and act like. But I never really understood it until I put it in the real-life context of my real-life body. And when I finally did understand that this definition applied to me—to all my lumps and cellulite and 3XL dresses—I realized feminism is more powerful than I had ever suspected.

And so am I. And so are you—you are more powerful than you know.

Anne Thériault

Ten AMAZING Scientists (Who Also Happen To Be Women)

1. **Ada Lovelace** (1815-1852) the world's first computer programmer (look up the Analytical Engine!)

2. **Mae Jemison** (born 1956) a NASA astronaut & the first African American woman to travel in space

3. **Maria Mayer** (1906-1972) winner of the Nobel Prize for proposing the nuclear shell model of the Atomic Nucleus

4. **Shirley Jackson** (born 1946) the first African American woman to earn a doctorate at MIT & also the inventor of the fiber optic cable.

5. **Lise Meitner** (1878-1968) the first person to hypothesize nuclear fission

6. **Annie Jump Cannon** (1863-1941) an astronomer instrumental in the development of stellar classification

7. **Caroline Herschel** (1750-1848) the first woman to discover a comet & the first woman to have her work published by the Royal Society.

8. **Sameera Moussa** (1917-1952) an Egyptian nuclear physicist who worked to make the medical use of nuclear technology affordable to all

9. **Rosalind Franklin** (1920-1958) helped discover the structure of DNA & RNA

10. **Hypatia** (circa AD 360-415) a mathematician, astronomer & philosopher; head of the Neoplatonic school in Alexandria, Egypt

Pretty Enough

BY ALIDA NUGENT

I told my mother I wanted a nose job when I was only fourteen years old.

I grew up in Westchester, New York, a suburb full of things like antiques shops, cider festivals, and designer purses. The people were a little friendly, a little suspicious. My high school was filled with rugby players, conservatives, and beautiful white girls.

I was not a beautiful white girl. I am biracial, and it shows! This made me feel confused most of the time, and I wasn't the only one: I'm half Puerto Rican and half Irish, but mostly I just look disorienting. I have very curly hair, but it's not coarse like my mother's. My nose burns in the sun, but I get very, very tan everywhere else. I look like every ethnicity that eats hummus or plantains, and people aren't afraid to shout various countries at me to try to figure out where I might be from: "Armenia!" "Greece!" "Cuba?!"

In my teenaged years, I experienced the curiously affectionate friendships of girls who didn't really understand me. They would tan in the sun after weeks spent at resorts in Jamaica or Mexico, returning to place their fading arms next to mine to compare our color. They would casually mention how dark the hair on my arms was. They would straighten my hair for me, which then "looked much better." I would pluck my eyebrows in the middle. I would smile in every picture, even as I tried to hide my stomach and growing breasts; while my friends were growing upward, I was growing outward. And if, like the *Sesame Street* song, one thing was not like the other, surely I was the one thing that did not belong.

But man, did I try. I dressed like them. I bought the perfumes they did. I borrowed their phrases and mannerisms. I *almost* looked like them. But I really didn't. I was darker, and heavier, and different. I could roll my *r*'s. I danced to salsa with my grandmother. I had odd ingredients in my kitchen like achiote seeds and sofrito paste from the mostly untouched international foods section of my local grocery store. I loved these girls because they were nice to me, and I loved them because they had freckles and rosy cheeks and all the other things I thought were beautiful. But we were different, and I couldn't shake it.

"Where are you from again?" They asked me this sometimes.

"The rain forest," I would say. *And my dad is from the Bronx,* I would think.

The thing I resented most about my appearance was my nose. It was the same nose my grandmother and grandfather and my other ancestors had—fat and squat and the first thing you noticed about me. I could wear the (knockoff) North Face jackets, but it was my nose that betrayed me. "Puerto Rican," it said to me. I didn't know if it said that to anyone else, but it sure said it to me. "Not white. Different." I hated it.

When I told my mother I wanted a nose job, to have the thin, upturned nose of all my friends, we were in the car. That way I didn't have to look at her face. The things I told her in the car were not good things: "I got a C on my math test"; "I forgot to call Grandma and thank her for the birthday gift"; "It would be great if you let me undergo major surgery to fix my weird little face."

My mother's answer: "You are beautiful."

I knew the good things about me. I had long eyelashes and was a good listener and could tell if a candle smelled good just by looking at it. But I was not beautiful. Beautiful was Ash, the most popular girl in school who had a nose that looked like it belonged on an elf. While standing in the grocery store checkout line, I saw pictures of famous women's nose jobs, and the magazines featured the new images as improvements. And even though I eventually learned that nobody is 100 percent happy with their face, I didn't know it then. All I *knew* was that I was the only "before" picture in town. I *knew* I was *not beautiful.* This seemed like a cold, hard, nonnegotiable fact. I repeated it to myself, often, so nobody could say it to me first.

I knew the importance of beauty. I knew that beautiful girls got dates, boyfriends, everything they wanted. But I also knew that *feeling* beautiful was what I wanted most of all so I could feel accepted, and comfortable, and happy. I wanted to sit in a room with my beautiful friends, and I wanted them to put their arms next to mine and say, "I wish I looked more like you."

For my sixteenth birthday, my family went to Puerto Rico to visit my grandfather. I hadn't been there since I was much younger. I didn't know what to expect.

Have you ever seen something or someone and immediately felt like you've never known life without them? It fills a place that's half-empty. It makes you feel like you've been missing something your whole life, and then all of a sudden, you're not missing it anymore.

That was Puerto Rico for me.

Everything about Puerto Rico was amazing. The houses painted in pastel colors, the coconut ice, the people who sold beaded necklaces out of tiny shops, the avocados and ocean and air that felt thick and salty and like it was always about to rain. The old men listening to radios on lawn chairs outside their houses, the secret sips from my mother's piña coladas, the lively music, and the little frogs that were unafraid of people and peppered the whole place with sound. My mother was happier—memories of her childhood made her cheeks flush as she told me about picking crabs from the beach and climbing trees and visiting all kinds of people.

But it was the *women* and the *girls* that blew me away. So many of them looked like me with wide noses, big saucer eyes, large breasts, short bodies, tiny hands, and hairy arms. They were in every store, every salon, every restaurant and mall. Girls who looked like me and thought I looked like them. It was another feeling I didn't know I missed until I felt it—feeling a part of something, feeling like you are not the odd one out, feeling like everyone else. And I would walk into shops with my curly hair cooperating beautifully in the thick, hot air, and the store owners would speak Spanish to me, and it was comfortable. And it was happy. And *I felt like me.*

It made me realize I never really wanted to look like my friends at all. They were beautiful, but it wasn't any specific trait that made them beautiful: it was that I felt like they were the only definition of pretty. I didn't mind having brown hair that puffed up in humidity. I didn't mind being darker and shorter. I just didn't want to feel so *alone*. The thing that I couldn't shake *wasn't* how fat my nose was, but instead how unwelcome I felt with it.

Belonging somewhere—feeling at home in your body, believing in yourself, and knowing who you are—that's what I was really missing when I longed to look like my classmates. When you want to be someone else, you can never be yourself or learn who you really are. I was dreaming of freckles instead of exploring my humor or learning to love and live and be wild and young and *myself.*

Puerto Rico didn't fix everything. I still thought my nose was fat. But I left knowing something new, and odd, and wonderful: there was a place for me in the world. There was a place for me in the world, even though I had a unibrow and yellowish skin and a fat stomach. I was not alone. I was present, and real, and here, and *me.*

And oh, how beautiful it is to feel just like yourself.

HELLO MY NAME IS LIZ PRINCE

FEMINIST

and I'm a Feminist!

But I wasn't always a feminist.

Behold: LIZ PRINCE, teenage misogynist

Pfft, girls. Whatever.

MISOGYNIST

Here are some common misconceptions about misogyny.

1. That girls can't be misogynists. Unfortunately, girls hating girls is incredibly prevalent, and in some cases, is even encouraged in our culture.

A trap that I easily fell into as a disgruntled tomboy who didn't fit in.

Everyone likes "real girls" and I'll never be one. I hate girls.

MISOGYNIST

2. That hating girls is a choice. We're bombarded by narratives that paint women as inferior to men, it's almost impossible not to absorb that message.

You've got to save me!

You're HYSTERICAL, woman!

ugh.

3. That a misogynist can never become a feminist. Evolving our politics and ideals as we grow and have new experiences is a big part of life.

REALIZATION

HOLY COW! I've been thinking about this all wrong! Girls aren't the enemy!

Sometimes change can feel like betrayal.

E tu, Brutus?

Oh, grow up already!

Sometimes we're even blind to our own changes.

I DON'T EVEN KNOW YOU ANYMORE!

Good.

I was talking to a friend a few weeks ago and she said:

I judge women way harsher than I do the men I encounter on the street.

Oh. I try not to judge other women at all.

I didn't realize this was true until I said it.

Because for so many years my default had been to dislike other women, the fact that I'd been able to alter my mindset felt like a big achievement. And it happened so gradually I didn't even notice!

Whoa! I really did change!

It's like I unexpectedly earned a new merit badge in my recovery from misogyny.

And I'm sure there are many more I have yet to earn.

Because I'm still growing and learning and evolving.

I'm just waiting for my next lightning strike.

I Have Always Eaten the Bread

BY LILY MYERS

I used to dread the bread basket moment. You know the one: the waiter sets down the appetizer of warm rolls in front of you, and you want nothing more than to take one. But you've been told, time and time again, that bread is a "bad" food. So the battle begins: will you eat the bread, or not?

I can't tell you how many accumulated hours of my life have been spent in this exact dilemma, whether it's with the bread basket, or the ice-cream cone, or any other food that's been labeled "bad." If you're like me, you have probably spent a large percentage of your life thinking about the shape that your body makes. I began to notice it in middle school. That's when my female peers and I started furtively comparing bodies: who had breasts, who didn't, who was tall, who was thin, and on and on. In some ways, it was largely natural female curiosity about our drastically changing figures. Huge changes were happening to our bodies; of course we were going to peek curiously at other girls' chests.

But I also remember certain insidious words creeping into our conversations. The first time I called myself "fat" was in sixth grade. I *knew* I wasn't fat, but I had picked up from somewhere that I was supposed to think I was. That same year, a friend called me "anorexic" during lunch. I knew it was supposed to be a compliment—she meant that I was skinny—and I took it as such. I didn't consider the destructive meaning behind that word, the fact that it refers to a terrible and sometimes lethal disease. I was just happy to be seen as skinny.

I never worried about my body until puberty. Then the changes hit, and with them came a rush of confusion. I was tall, suddenly, and with the new height came *more* of me. For the first time I felt large, and I hated it. We are constantly told, in the media and in popular culture, that the ideal of femaleness is smallness. While men are told to bulk *up*, women are told to slim *down*.

So I began to try to achieve this ideal. I became increasingly aware of what I allowed into my body. This hyperawareness reached its peak in my early college years, when it morphed into full-on obsession. I remember going home for the summer after my freshman year, so sad to leave this new place I loved, and thinking, *Oh well, at least I have a project.*

Losing weight: that was my "project." And it quickly consumed me. It was a game of endless subtraction: if I was better off eating *half* a bagel instead of a full bagel, then surely I was better off eating none of it at all! It was an addictive game, reinforced by constant feelings of guilt or pride. If I'd gone a day barely eating anything, I felt pretty and successful. If I "messed up"—eating the bread, for instance—I felt an overwhelming guilt that would last for days.

Where did this guilt come from? When did I learn that maintaining a thin body was so essential to my being? I'll never be able to pinpoint the exact source of this destructive idea, because the sad truth is that we are steeped in it. In myriad ways, our culture tells women and girls that we are valued most highly for our appearance. We are barraged with the message that our worth is inextricably linked to the shapes that our bodies make.

Have you ever waited in the checkout line at the grocery store and stared at the rack of glossy magazine covers featuring women with flawless skin, flat stomachs, and impossibly toned thighs? This used to make me feel so bad about myself. Because I will never look like that. And to have these images pasted on the cover of every magazine drives home the message that this is the one, singular version of beauty. That this is what it means to be an attractive woman, and that we all must aspire to this ideal. Must buy the magazines, must work out, must cut out the "bad" foods, and must constantly, impossibly, do better.

But here's the thing. The static, glossy images on the cover of those magazines? They're not *real*. I don't just mean that they're intensely photoshopped, though of course they are. I mean that they're not living, breathing humans like you and me. They are snapshots; tiny moments frozen in time and then drastically altered on the computer. In real life we don't exist that way. We grow and change every day of our lives. We are organic matter. We intake and output energy; we consume fuel so we can exist in the world of activities and thought and creativity and play. This means that the idea of ever "attaining" the perfect body is actually nonsensical. To aspire to the magazine-cover body is to aspire to stay forever still, frozen in time, looking out at the world from a stationary metal rack.

This realization was vital for me in finally breaking out of the toxic cycles of food control and guilt. I began to view my body not as a final product, but as a tool that allowed me to do what I love in the world: to play guitar and dance and hug my friends. I developed a mantra that I'd say to myself whenever I was feeling uneasy: *This is the shape that my body makes today.* It emphasized that every day my body would look and feel slightly different. And it reminded me that my body was my home. The place where I had always and would always live. I no longer wanted to be locked in a vicious battle with my own home.

I also came to realize just how much time and mental energy I was spending on controlling my body. For many months, I'd write down "lose weight" or "stay skinny" in a list of goals every morning and night. I'd plan my entire day around these goals. I thought I was practicing self-improvement; it turned out to be more like self-imprisonment. My brain was a tetherball, constantly pulled back to the scrutiny of my body. It was completely exhausting, and it also just made me *sad*. I'd remember, with a pang, the years when I was unmoored by this mental trap, when my thoughts could move as freely as they wanted.

Admitting to myself that I had an obsession was hard, but it allowed me to realize that I wanted to become untethered. I didn't want my entire life to be a weight-loss strategy. I wanted to concentrate on my passions and interests and friends. I wanted to actually engage in conversations over lunch instead of monitoring every bite. Getting lost in the bread-basket dilemma makes it impossible to truly pay attention to the world.

The secret I finally learned is this: it doesn't matter if you eat the bread. It never does. What matters is how much of your mind is devoted to this terrible cycle. It's never-ending; even if you "achieve" the body you want, the obsession doesn't end. Even when I liked my body's shape, I was still preoccupied with maintaining it, terrified that I might lose it. So there's no way to win, except to exit the cycle altogether.

None of this is our fault. We are told constantly in the media that it is our paramount responsibility to keep ourselves thin. And this is why body image is a feminist issue. This "responsibility" to keep our bodies perfect is a narrative told to females. Yes, men can feel insecurity about their bodies, too. But the same level of importance is not attached to body image for men. Women and girls are constantly told, both overtly and subtly, that their very *worth* is connected to their fulfillment of a narrow ideal of physical beauty.

Want proof? Look at the covers of those aforementioned magazines. Whereas women's magazines feature articles—almost exclusively—about appearance ("Lose Ten Pounds Fast!" "Get Your Best Beach Body!"), men's magazines feature articles about men actually *doing* things in the world. This illustrates the systemic imbalance in how the genders are taught to measure their success. Women are taught to measure it by the number on the scale. Men are taught to measure it by their accomplishments and achievements.

Refusing to buy into this body obsession is therefore a feminist act. The personal is political. When I choose to love my body, to look at it with compassion and remember all the awesome things it can do, *I am rebelling against a system that wants to keep me down.* I am actively protesting the status quo that aims to keep me self-obsessed, self-critical, and self-oppressing.

Disavowing body obsession is also a political act because it refuses to pay money and time to a billion-dollar "beauty" industry that benefits directly from women's insecurity. Ads and commercials aim to make us doubt ourselves, so we'll spend money on products. Every time we give money to these companies, we are feeding an industry that will never let us feel secure.

It's easy to forget this political aspect, because body image feels so personal to us. We go to great lengths to hide our body-image struggles. I remember using excuses—"Oh, I've already eaten," or "Oh, I just don't like ice cream"—rather than admitting that I was going through a phase of body obsession. Because that's part of maintaining the façade of perfection, too, right? Not only wanting the perfect body, but also not wanting to admit the lengths we go to in order to achieve it. And this can be very, very lonely. What if women and girls were more open about body insecurity—would it be easier to remember that this is, in fact, a political issue? Could we band together in this fight to love our bodies?

To move from obsession to body love is difficult. You can't just flip a switch and instantly forget the body image pressure. But you can remind yourself, day after day, that loving your body is revolutionary, feminist, and empowering. You can remind yourself that your worth is not tied to the number on the scale. And consistently reminding yourself of these things *does* make an enormous difference. Thanks to neuroplasticity, our brains are malleable; the more we think about things in a certain way, the more we will default to that way of thinking. If I tell myself I'm beautiful every day, this thought becomes easier, even automatic. And this process, after years of body criticism, feels *so* good.

Starting this journey wasn't easy for me. I had to relinquish the desire for perfection and become a realist instead. Because here's the thing: I have always eaten the bread. Whenever the basket arrived, no matter how much I internally yelled at myself, I'd always reach for the rolls. The inner parts of me were always too much at war: the part that wanted the perfect stomach and thighs, and the part that just wanted to let it all go, to surrender, to bite into the thick crust of a just-baked loaf.

I'm happy to say the latter half won. It's an ongoing process; I still scrutinize my body, and I have to remind myself to stop. But I've learned, finally, that to accept imperfection is to set myself free. That to release control is to allow myself to fully enjoy life. Now I can get dinner with my friends and listen to what they're saying, without drowning them out with my critical inner monologue. I can go swimming and finally stop sucking in my stomach. I can float out into the water, able to concentrate on the feeling of the infinite world around me, instead of my body's shape.

Women are humans. Complete, complex, flawed, beautiful, worthy humans. So to expect an impossible level of perfection from ourselves is, in fact, self-oppression. It's denying ourselves the pleasure and privilege of being *real*. To allow ourselves the freedom and joy of being imperfect humans is a feminist act. To let go of obsession is to make room for self-love. And for women in this world, self-love is radical. Radical, joyful, and as delicious as that first bite of fresh-baked bread.

BAD HAIR DAY by Stasia Burrington

Dragging Myself into Self-Love

BY CONSTANCE AUGUSTA ZABER

When I was a kid, I stole blush from my grandmother because I was tired of hating how I looked. I hated my cheekbones, my eyes, my forehead, my hair. I hated whatever it was that made people look at me and say, "That child is *male*." All I wanted was to alter my appearance and tweak my face so that people would look at me and say, "That child is *female*."

Early in life, I identified makeup as a potential solution to my woes. I grew up watching my grandmother put on her makeup. She would apply her lipstick and blush with careful deliberation, using small movements that hypnotized me. I began to think that if makeup allowed my grandmother to highlight her natural beauty, maybe it could do the same for me. I could see the power makeup gave my grandmother, the way it helped her gain confidence, and I hoped that power might help me, too.

So I stole a tiny container of her blush. The exact details of this crime are hazy to me now, but I was about ten years old, and I probably lifted it while looking in her purse for hard candies. The only detail I'm completely clear on is that I was acting out of a frustration that I couldn't put into words. I was so frustrated, so tired of feeling hurt by my own body, that the only thing I could think of doing was to steal from my grandmother.

For years, that blush remained hidden in my room. At this point in my life, everyone around me believed I was a boy, which meant that I was absolutely not allowed to have anything to do with makeup. As liberal and progressive as my family could be, I was still living in a town in which gender roles were policed with fervor. Any boy deviating from his gender role could expect to be descended upon by his classmates, particularly by boys whose own insecurities made them especially cruel. If I really was a boy, then my makeup could never see the light of day.

On the rare occasions when I was convinced no one would come into my room and discover my secret, I would take out the blush. I loved to sweep the bristles of its tiny brush through the powder that shimmered like a pink pearl. Sometimes I would even put it on my cheeks, but the instant I looked into the mirror, I would feel sick. The blush that looked so delicate and pretty on my grandmother only made my ugliness more obvious. The sickness I felt, the betrayal and the pain, would turn to anger, and I would tell myself that I was going to throw it away. In the end, however, my belief in its power would win out. The blush would go back into the drawer until enough time had passed for me to forget how hurt I had been, and I would try again.

In middle school, I gave up hope of ever loving how I looked. As the girls around me began to try out new styles, I buried myself inside the same old clothes I'd always worn. Looking back, I can recognize how hard puberty must have been for them, but at the time, I envied those girls. I envied their pierced ears, their lip gloss, their long hair, their shoes that weren't boring old sneakers. I was envious that they were allowed to make choices with clothes and makeup that were off-limits to me. By the eighth grade, I'd been exposed to the idea that gender roles were created by humans and were more arbitrary than natural (thank you, Internet!), but that sort of abstract information is useless in the face of classmates who would mock a boy for having a purple backpack.

In the darkness of high school, there was one shining moment, a single shining night that came once a year: drag night.

How does a teenager who doesn't have a car, who lives in the middle of nowhere, and who is socially isolated end up involved in drag? Through her parents, of course.

My parents both worked at a small college, and when I was in eighth grade, one of their students organized a drag show to celebrate Pride Week on campus. I listened to their description of the night, trying to absorb every detail. Although I was still completely in denial about being trans, I couldn't stop thinking about this magical event where it was okay for men to wear dresses and makeup and (pretend to) be girls. I was obsessed. When I found out there would be another drag show the following year, I convinced my sister to not just go with me, but to also help me prepare for performing in the competition.

The night of the show, my sister gave me my first proper makeover. When I saw myself in the mirror with eyeliner and mascara and red lips, I wanted to cry. But unlike my tears over the disastrous blush experiments, these were tears of joy. With makeup on my face, I liked my reflection in the mirror. I couldn't stop looking at myself.

That night I floated around the lecture hall that had been done up as a performance space. I wasn't only enjoying the way the blue dress moved as I walked or how the eyeliner made my eyes sparkle; I was riding high, knowing that, for a night, I was a girl. When people looked at me and used a traditionally female name or referred to me as "she" and "her," I was beyond thrilled. That drag show was the first time I felt like I had come close to honestly expressing who I was, both to the world and to myself. Sure, the makeup my sister had used on me was very much *her* style, bold colors that I wouldn't have chosen for myself, but I'd seen how the world had changed for me.

More important, I had seen my reflection and recognized the girl in the mirror.

My sister and I ended up coming in second that night, but the real victory was when my cousin commented on a Facebook picture from that night, saying I was a "pretty girl."

I started my college life in one of America's smallest cities, but compared to the rural cow town I was from, it might as well have been Manhattan. Free of the eyes of my community back home, I started wearing the clothing that I couldn't have worn in high school. Slowly, my wardrobe changed from jeans and big T-shirts to secondhand dresses and cheap high heels. This transition helped me feel more connected with my body, but I remained at odds with my face. I started buying hordes of cheap makeup from the drugstore, but since I never had anyone to teach me what to do with it, my attempts at makeup more complicated than lipstick and mascara could reduce me to tears. At the time, I took these struggles as a cosmic sign that makeup was to remain out of my hands and in the realm of women.

In my second year of college, two decades' worth of repression caught up with me to produce a fairly spectacular breakdown. The next few years had me leaving college, moving to a new state, being unemployed, starting at a new college, and then getting kicked out of school because I was too depressed to do my homework. During this mess, however, I was finally able to stop believing the lie that I was a man and began to tell everyone that they were wrong and that I was a woman.

I take a certain amount of pleasure in being able to tell people that they're wrong.

I wish I could say that coming out as a transsexual woman was similar to emerging from the fires of my life like a phoenix to fly above my struggles, but that would be far from accurate. Coming out saved my life, but it certainly didn't solve all my problems. I still fight daily with my depression and anxiety, and I now face new challenges like hiring discrimination, fighting with bureaucracy to update government documents, and some really charming street harassment.

But even though coming out allowed me to stop lying to myself and to start living, I still struggle with how I look in the mirror. The only thing that comes close to making me feel good is makeup. Makeup empowers me. I have tools to work with the reflection that used to make me feel helpless. Instead of pretending that I don't have a face, I now know its minute details. I consider my skin tone, identify specific areas I'm uncomfortable with, and see the features I love and want to highlight for the world. Instead of just thinking, *Ugh, I hate how I look*, I now ask myself, *What don't I like, and what am I able to do about it?*

It's taken me many years, but I'm beginning to learn that makeup doesn't have any sort of mystic power by itself. Makeup may not be a magic potion, but for me it's an important ingredient in the potion. The careful use of makeup brings me back into my body and allows me to go out in public without obsessing over whether or not people are staring at my dark stubble, and instead tell myself that they're staring at the cheekbones I've lovingly highlighted with the same blush I jacked from my grandma all those years ago. Makeup alleviates some of my daily pain, freeing up emotional space in my life so I can keep on fighting the root causes of the violence and oppression and marginalization I see around me.

Every so often, I hear someone comment that wearing makeup isn't feminist because it's all about appealing to the male gaze and supports the sexualization of women. I don't entirely buy that argument. My makeup is all about me. Makeup helps to keep me safe and find joy in my appearance. Makeup reminds me that I get to define what pretty looks like for me, reminding me that I love my cheekbones and my lower lip and the fact that my dark thick eyebrows underscore my emotions.

Makeup allows me to meet my eyes in the mirror.

CHAPTER three

GENDER,

Sex & Sexuality

SLUT. Prude. PLAYER. STUD. WHORE.

These are just a few of the words you'll hear tossed around when describing people who choose to have—or not to have—sex.

They each carry different connotations, as if someone's choice about sex is anyone else's business. As if their sex lives determine their worth or status.

He. She. Ze. They. Hir. Queer. Trans. A.

Feminists can identify as female, male, transgender, gender queer, or any other way they wish to. They can choose to choose no identity at all or choose one identity today and a different one next week. What physical parts individuals have or do not have has no bearing on their feminism nor on their right to be part of the feminism party. All that matters is that they believe in equality for every individual.

Whether you identify as a trans man, move fluidly among genders, enjoy having sex freely, or prefer not to have sex at all, you belong here and you matter. Your voice, your stories, your experiences—you deserve them, and you deserve to share them as loudly or quietly as you wish.

The Likability Rule

BY COURTNEY SUMMERS

The page is blank. There's a story I want to tell.

I have a girl in mind for it.

She'll be a difficult girl.

She'll be a difficult girl, not necessarily because I planned her that way, but because after writing and publishing five books, I know.

I know that we live in a world where *Girls are made of sugar and spice and everything nice* is less a suggestion, more an expectation, and at worst, a demand. *Girls must be* gentle, selfless, self-effacing, uncertain, quiet, and deferential. *Girls should* not wear too much of this or too little of that. Girls are not expected to lead (businesses, households, and governments) or have any say over their own bodies. There is no shortage of ways we police girls on how to *be*.

If you're a girl, you'll understand this the first time you live and breathe outside the lines because someone will always have something to say about it when you do.

In my books, the girls live and breathe outside the lines. My books are about girls coping with pain and trauma. They are navigating, to the best of their abilities, cruel and hostile landscapes including mean girls, mean boys, depression, death, suicide and sexual violence, to name a few.

Their pain is a dark room they find themselves in from the very first sentence on the very first page, and every sentence and page after that, I have them search for a way out. They'll reach a door. I'll have them run their hands along its edges. They'll fight their way through.

The girls in my books always fight their way through.

But what if, when the girl opens the door, she's suddenly in another room, and in this room, there's an audience? They've been waiting, secretly watching her the whole time. Some will have connected to her struggle; others won't—fiction is subjective, after all. And then there are others still, the ones who say, "I understand she went through hell to be here, but she could have been more *likable* about it."

In fiction, likability rules.

Or, The Likabilty Rule:

```
A female character must be likable above
   all else, lest she sacrifice the ideal.
```

Unfortunately, emotional pain and trauma contradict the primary Sugar and Spice tenets of Being a Girl. Nothing about pain is *likable*. It's often harsh, selfish, all-consuming, alienating, loud and ugly. A girl in pain can be all of these things at once, but if she is, that means she certainly sacrifices the ideal, and let's face it: a girl who isn't nice isn't nice to read *about*.

If a female character breaks the likability contract with some readers—and doesn't spend the rest of the book apologizing for it—she forfeits their sympathy and support. An unlikable female character is not worthy of their time, compassion, empathy, or kindness.

She's not even worth the time, compassion, empathy and kindness of other *characters*.

In 2015, I released a book called *All the Rage.* It's about a girl named Romy, who is raped by the local sheriff's son. His family is powerful. Hers is not. She lives on the wrong side of town. He doesn't. He's the Golden Boy. She's far from the Golden Girl. When word of the accusation gets out, her entire town turns against her. She's branded a liar—the Girl Who Cried Rape.

The book is not only about Romy coming to terms with her rape, but having to do so in front of a merciless audience who finds it safer and easier not to believe her. Every time Romy makes a mistake, acts questionably, or (especially) does something unlikable in response to her trauma, they find it even *easier* to not believe her.

The rape culture she lives in has devastating and far-reaching consequences.

There's also a thread of romance in the book. Romy catches the eye of a boy she works with named Leon. Leon's interest in Romy is initially superficial; Romy wears red lipstick and nail polish as armor because her appearance is one of the few things in her life she can control. He's intrigued by that. Romy likes Leon, too. He's the first boy she's developed feelings for since she was raped.

But Romy is suffering from post-traumatic stress disorder, and it's hard for her to reconcile what happened in her past with what she wants for her future. Leon lives a town over and doesn't know what happened to her. She never wants him to find out because his not knowing offers Romy a reprieve from being the Girl Who Cried Rape.

Over the course of the novel, it becomes increasingly difficult for Romy to keep those two selves separate. She messes up a lot with Leon, and he stays with her because . . .

"Why? Why would he ever?"

This is a question I've seen many times in the wake of the book's publication, and it's often followed by statements such as, "I don't understand why or how Leon would be with a girl so difficult and unlikable."

Romy broke the Likability Rule and, in doing so, made herself unworthy of Leon's romantic interest and the reader's support.

And it's true: Romy is difficult. She acts in haste. She's not always nice. She can be unlikable, just like anybody has the potential to be. She's also traumatized. The best she's capable of offering Leon—and in spite of all she's going through, she *is* trying her best—still falls much too short for some readers.

Romy is not even worthy of Leon's love on *Leon's* terms. These same readers can't accept that Leon realizes Romy is struggling but that she's trying in spite of it. That she's trying is not a good enough reason for him to make an emotional commitment or to want to help her. It doesn't matter that Leon calls her out on the hurt she causes him—which was important to me, because while Romy *is* going through a lot, it doesn't give her free license to treat people badly. The demands placed on him are too great for her to deserve all of the good he offers. For Leon to be with Romy requires work on *his* part, and because of that, she's not at all worthy of his love.

Juxtapose this against the fact that we have so many unquestioned and accepted narratives about *male* characters who hurt and use girls to cope with their own pain, who are lauded for their emotional depth and complexity. It doesn't matter if they are nice to female characters; they are allowed to be *complicated*—just like real people happen to be.

It seems as long as a character can personally benefit from or is rewarded for giving their time and love to an Unlikable Girl, we accept she's deserving of it. If the benefits of loving her are less clearly defined and with fewer tangible rewards, she is not.

It's okay to want to like the female characters you read about, and it's okay if you don't; but it's worth taking a closer look at what your definitions of "likable" and "unlikable" are, because you might be surprised at what this reveals. Do your definitions change depending on whether you're reading about a female or male character?

And if so, how so?

It's critical we examine the kind of standards we hold fictional girls to and consider how it reflects in the way we treat *real* girls and, most important, what kind of emotional impact that has on them. What are we saying to girls when we cannot accept difficult, hurting female characters as being worthy of love *because* they are difficult and hurting?

Are we telling them they have to hide their pain and act likable to be loved?

Over the course of my career, I've heard from many girls who confide in me that they are or have been the difficult, *unlikable* female characters I write about. They tell me what they've lived through and live with. They tell me they're relieved to see themselves on the page, not only because it validates their experiences, but also because they feel less alone in those moments where they "failed" to live up to our deeply ingrained societal expectations of being a girl. These are female readers who did not feel they were allowed to acknowledge their hurt or work through it, because it wasn't a *nice* thing to do, and they've felt that pressure to be nice and likable their whole lives, even if it's at the expense of themselves.

A world that denies female characters emotional complexity for the sole purpose of making their stories palatable is a world that tells real girls they only matter conditionally. But when we recognize and acknowledge the unique struggles and challenges girls face on a daily basis as important, we show girls that *they* are important. When we show girls they matter, we empower them, and an empowered girl can do *anything* she puts her mind to. She can raise her voice against social injustice. Start a movement. Win a Nobel Prize. Shatter glass ceilings. Change the world.

She can develop the tools to be there for and empower other girls.

As a reader, do you consider it more important that the girls you meet in books are likable, or is it more important for you to let go of that expectation and understand that the sole purpose of a girl's existence is not to always be liked above all else?

I write about difficult, angry, hurting and *unlikable* girls, and I imagine I always will, and the difficult, angry, hurting and unlikable girls in my books will always, *always*, have people who care about and love them. And, in writing these books, I suppose I will always reach that inevitable point where readers ask me to defend that decision. But why should I?

I will never perpetuate the idea that a girl's pain isn't worthy of anyone's time, patience, understanding, compassion, empathy or love, or that receiving these things depends on how likable and nice she is. Ever. I reject the Likability Rule because I see girls beyond the limits society places on them. Because a girl should never have to hide her pain and act likable to be worthy and deserving of all good things. Because it's not a hurting girl's responsibility to convince us. Because it's our responsibility to let her know.

Girls, you are worthy and deserving of all good things.

You are, you are, you are.

Broken Body, Worthless Girl, and Other Lies I Called the Truth

BY KAYLA WHALEY

Dear Kayla,

I've been thinking about you a lot lately. I know it's not mutual—anything past age twenty seems like a lifetime away to you, and in some ways it is—but I miss you. I miss your certainty that you can do anything you want, even if you don't know what that is yet. I miss the easy smile you offer strangers as though it costs you nothing. I miss your endless hope.

Well, not *endless*. You are only human, despite the way others expect you to be pure of heart and strong of spirit, as though your wheelchair were a talisman imbuing you with some saintly essence. They foist their surety on you the way the fairies bestowed their gifts upon Aurora: "You are innocent, you are pure, you are good." You nod and thank them. What else can you do?

Do you remember when you first realized you were broken? I don't. I was just me. Different than the other kids, sure, but I must have made the leap from "different" to "worse" at some point. Maybe it wasn't a leap, though. It's not such a great distance from one to the other when you're small and the world is big. (The world is still big, I hate to say, but you are, too.) Maybe it was no farther than the space between breaths. As I said, I don't remember.

It doesn't much matter, anyway. The point is, you were broken and you knew it, but you also didn't because you were just you. You had a beautiful smile (everyone said so) and hair like spun gold (at least according to the bus monitor that one time). You liked to wear Dr Pepper Lip Smacker, and one day you started wondering if other people liked you wearing it, too. You wondered if boys liked it. If they noticed your beautiful smile and golden hair. You figured they must, because they noticed the other girls.

But you weren't like other girls, were you?

Other girls didn't have two metal rods screwed into their spines to keep them straight. They didn't lean to the right constantly, their clothes always off-center. They didn't dance with a head bob and some jerky arm movements. They didn't drag along several hundred pounds of wheelchair everywhere.

Other girls were beautiful.

Other girls were *desirable*.

You learned early (so very early) that desirability was the goal. It didn't matter that you liked your reflection if boys didn't like it, too. You came up with so many scenarios for your first kiss: by a lake under the full moon, during a study session after school, in a dark movie theater. You'd create these mini-plays, arranging the sets and fleshing out character motivations, but you never made it to the climax. When the big moment came, you couldn't work out the logistics—Would he be sitting, too? Standing bent over? Would your chair get in the way? Of course it would; your chair always gets in the way—and so you ended the fantasy early.

In some ways, it was easier to fantasize about sex. You had no idea how that worked even for able-bodied people, so you mostly replayed sex scenes from movies in your head. Sometimes you'd insert yourself in the scene, sometimes not. You felt guilty either way. You'd touch yourself, but it was always fast and quiet and hard to enjoy. After, you'd worry you had done it wrong, and then you'd worry that it was wrong to do at all.

You didn't know if other girls masturbated (I can tell you now that many of them definitely did), but you knew no one expected *you* to do so. Your body was broken, after all. You weren't interested in sex, surely. Not you who were so innocent and pure and good. You still wanted to be those things, and you were terrified someone would find out you weren't.

It didn't help that all your closest friends in high school were devoutly

Christian. They were waiting until marriage. Sure, they might talk about their crushes or whichever male celebrity was popular, but then they'd pray together for their future husbands. You'd all gather in a circle, hands clasped, heads bowed, and say, "Jesus, we pray for the men you'll bring into our lives one day. We pray that they've stayed away from temptation. We pray that you'll prepare our hearts for them and help us keep our bodies pure for them. Amen." You said those words, too, but you didn't mean them. Not because you wanted to have sex before marriage (you didn't, but oh, you also did), but because you knew there was no husband in your future. It wasn't a conscious knowing—you hoped someone would find you attractive someday—but the kind of knowing that fizzes under your skin.

You're about to start college now, aren't you? About to move out for the first time, live on your own, make new friends and take new classes. I can tell you it'll be even better than you hope, but that's not the whole story. (It rarely is.)

Your very first semester, you'll fall hard and fast for one of your new best friends. He'll be intelligent and passionate, and you'll laugh more than you ever have before. Maybe even more important, he'll flirt with you. You won't realize it at first, but soon you'll notice the way he looks at you as though you two share a secret. You'll notice how he sits close sometimes and brushes against you. You'll notice how his voice changes when he jokes with you, and how your voice changes, too. You'll worry this is all in your head, but that won't stop you from hoping. This is college; anything could happen, right? Maybe here you aren't broken.

Maybe here you're just like the other girls.

I'm sorry. I'm sorry to tell you the rest of this story, because it's going to hurt to hear. It'll hurt even more to experience, though, so maybe knowing it's coming will soften the impact.

You'll go dancing one night. You'll spend forever getting ready because he'll be going, too. He's never gone with the group before. You'll put on your makeup and imagine the dark, crowded club, wondering if it'll feel different with him there, so close.

You'll be pleased with yourself that night. You won't worry even once about how you look dancing, because you know you're gorgeous tonight, and you feel too good to care about anything beyond the music pulsing through your body and his smile in the dark.

After, the group will head back to the dorms. You'll all congregate in his room, like usual, still sweaty and smelling like smoke and beer (which none of you drank, but it's a sticky scent). Someone will ask him if he had a good time. He'll shrug and say, "It was fine, but the ratio was off." Ratio? What ratio? He'll explain: "There were more guys in our group than girls."

There weren't, you'll think.

"There weren't," you'll say. "Four girls, four guys."

"Yeah," he'll say, "but you don't count."

You don't count. You aren't like the other girls. You don't count. Your body is different, broken, worthless. You are. You are worthless. You don't count.

You always knew, but no one had ever said it before. It was a truth you kept hidden even from yourself most of the time, a static you could pretend to ignore. No one had ever said it, but now someone does.

I didn't know how much it could hurt to be right.

Maybe I can spare you that moment. Maybe I can get to you first, now that I know the truth: he was wrong, and so were you.

You are not broken. There is nothing wrong with your body. You are beautiful and desirable, and those are not the most important things you are. You are worth more than all the stars and all the galaxies and all the mysteries of the universe combined.

You count.

You matter.

I love you.

I want to tell you another story now, if I may. You're sitting in Starbucks, waiting. You look up anxiously every time someone walks in, and then let out a disappointed, stuttering breath. Until one time you look up and there she is, your date. "Kayla?" she asks. You nod. She sits down, smiling and beautiful. She buys you coffee, and you worry the whole time that your carefully applied lipstick is rubbing off, probably smearing all across your face. You laughingly mention your concern. Later, she texts you: *i wanted to kiss the rest of that lipstick off you.*

You go on only one more date with her—turns out you weren't such a great fit. You never do kiss her, but she wanted to and you chose not to. You've never felt more powerful.

You're going to learn a lot in the coming years. You're bisexual, for one thing, although you won't figure that out or quite what it means until your early-to-mid-twenties. You'll discover a passion for writing, a joy in creating something from nothing except words and intention. You'll finally master eyeliner.

You'll find feminism, a word that is so much more than its few syllables. You'll marvel at the way it feels to say, "I am a feminist." Like both the bravest of declarations and nothing more than the most basic of truths.

I am: my life.

A feminist: has value.

You'll learn to love yourself. It won't be easy, but it will be worth it. Of course, sometimes you'll still look in the mirror and wonder how anyone could ever want to touch you, but then you'll remember two things:

i wanted to kiss the rest of that lipstick off you

and

I count. I matter.

Love,

Me

FAQs ABOUT FEMINISM

Is there a difference between "sex" and "gender"?

"Sex" and "gender" are different. "Sex" refers to the biological differences between people, including reproductive systems and other physiological sex characteristics. A person's sex is typically assigned at birth.

"Gender" refers to the identity an individual chooses to take, if they choose to take one at all. Gender can be known at a young age and remain the same throughout a person's life, or it can change at any time. The only person who chooses their gender identity and what it is or is not is the individual.

"Cis" gender individuals are those whose assigned sex matches their gender. Individuals whose sex does not match their gender may be trans (a person who identifies as a gender different from the one that corresponds to their sex at birth), intersex (a person whose sexual anatomy at birth doesn't fit the typical binary notions of male and female), gender fluid (someone whose gender identity varies over time), queer (a term that any individual who does not identify as heterosexual or cis gender may decide to use), or any other identity they feel best fits their life.

All the Bodies

BY RAFE POSEY

Once upon a time, I was a girl, more or less. I was not very good at it. This is not such a surprise, I guess, since I am, in fact, a boy. Trying to be a girl was exhausting and confusing, but transition seemed abstract and nearly impossible. Sometimes I just wanted to give up and forget about being transgender. Authenticity, as much as I craved it, was too elusive, and too hard to organize.

Eventually, after decades of suppressing my truth, I did manage to transition, and now I am a man of a certain age (do we describe men this way?). Also, I am a much better feminist now than I ever was before.

When I was trying to live as a woman, I eschewed the label "feminist." I would explain that I thought women should be equal, but I wasn't, you know, a feminist.

The main problem was that I wasn't angry, or rather I wasn't angry about what I thought of as feminist issues. I was very angry about the swirl of ideas in my own head about who I knew myself to be versus who I appeared to be to everyone else. And if I wasn't angry about the things feminists were angry about, clearly I couldn't be one, right?

I was wrong.

Part of my problem was that I had friends who embraced the label "feminist," and some of them believed terrible things about transgender people. They argued against the inclusion of trans women in women's spaces. They didn't understand trans issues, and in some cases, I'm pretty sure they didn't want to. I knew they were wrong. But what I only halfway understood was that their vision of what feminism was, and who it should include, was too narrow.

When I began my transition from she to he, I didn't understand that there are all kinds of ways that trans is a feminist issue, or that feminism is a trans issue: So much of what makes being trans harder revolves around issues like body autonomy and self-determination, around violence and public safety and being told what you "should" be. But "should," it turns out, is a giant crock. It's easy to say to someone else: you should wear this, or look like this, or have this kind of hair, or eat these things, or use this restroom, or be this size. You should be quiet. You should stop making a fuss. You should stop making the rest of us look bad. You should smile.

Recently, in my writing class, I asked my students to read the glorious Langston Hughes essay "My Adventures as a Social Poet." We talked at length about the purpose of such an essay, about what Hughes may have been trying to accomplish—who his audience may have been and the context in which he was writing. He lays it all out: "This is why I do not write poems about moonlight and roses. These are the reasons why I write poems about being the kind of man I am in the kind of country I inhabit. These are the reasons I am a social poet." I don't think Hughes was interested in the "should," or in being quiet.

We each have it in us to be a social poet of one sort or another. Right now, we live in a world where it's considered reasonable behavior to silence girls if what they're saying challenges the status quo. If a teenage girl says that an adult man at, say, a fandom convention, said or did something inappropriate to her, there is often an assumption that she's looking for attention, or is just plain wrong. And yet, girls keep stepping up and speaking out. Women of all ages keep coming forward to say, "This is not okay," despite constant waves of online harassment (or worse) by would-be silencers fueled by Gamergate, Islamophobia, racism, misogyny, or other hatreds.

The immediate cost of this is apparent—ravening legions who attack women all over the Internet, who dox women and create havoc and danger. The longer view, however, makes me hopeful. I was not especially brave when I was trying to live as a girl or as a woman, but I look at young women now—young women of all races, faiths, gender identities and expressions, abilities, learning styles, neurologies, sizes, orientations, all kinds of young women seething with energy and anger and the need to make change—and I feel hope. In my experience, you need a certain amount of hope to be trans, however you do or do not decide to transition. To some extent, modern feminism works the same way—it has to change, one way or another, from the insular models that preceded it. And that change requires the hope of new, innovative, young feminists coming up to keep those changes happening. As a trans man, I feel especially optimistic, because I look at how comfortable teens and young adults are now with their trans and genderfluid and non-binary friends, and it makes me want to weep with relief.

If I ask myself what I, a trans man, can do for feminism, I keep coming back to my ability to remind people that we are more than the skin in which we're born and the labels people attach to us. Some of those labels are a mistake, well-intentioned or otherwise, and sometimes they are the cruelest sort of trickery and gaslighting. Real feminism is about real equality, about the humanity present in all of us. And then I remember my friends talking about trans women all those years ago, and different friends much more recently explaining to me that I would be welcome in their women-only spaces, because I was kind of like a lesbian—but that trans women would not be. (I am actually not any kind of lesbian, what with being a man and all.) Bastions of modern feminism such as women's colleges like Smith and Barnard announced only as late as spring 2015 that they would accept applications from trans women. Many trans people struggle to get friends, family, coworkers, schools, and other institutions to stop using the names on their birth certificates (a lot of trans people call this their deadname, and they use that term for a reason).

When you deny a person his or her or hir name, or when you say, "You are not the kind of woman I recognize as a woman," you are also saying, "Hey, you there—who you know yourself to be is less important than who I need you to be." When you deny a person's lived experience, you are denying that person's right and ability to own his or her or hir narrative. You are denying that person's humanity, and that is not what feminism should be.

I keep coming back to empathy and to the incredible power it holds. By recognizing someone else's life and amplifying their voice, you are celebrating their humanity. And when you do that, you make it harder for the status quo to flourish. I am a trans man, but that is not the most important thing about me. I also really like cooking breakfast, and I have a soft spot for mystery novels. Sometimes when I'm in an old stone building, I wonder about the stories contained in the walls.

I believe to my core that true feminism is an unshakable and unstoppable force. The best kind of feminist—the best kind of human—embraces every woman, because if you narrow the perspective of what kind of women can be feminists, or what kind of women feminism should help, you're standing in the path of substantive change.

As a trans person, I am a constant example that our worlds and our lives can undergo and survive unfathomable change. Mine certainly did. As a result, transgender and gender-nonconforming people have a lot to offer modern feminism. Much of feminism right now revolves around bodily autonomy, about a woman's right to make her own decisions about her body, and the constant struggle against entrenched structural forces, such as anti-choice or anti-LGBTQ legislators. Likewise, we can't talk about trans without talking about bodily autonomy, including even the freedom to use the restroom without fear. Some people seem to think there is nothing more interesting in the world than a trans person's body. In the same way that some people blithely touch a pregnant person's belly, or legislate the functions of a uterus, they think it's their business what my body is like. Questions most cisgender people would never in a million years ask one another are often presumed to be fair game with trans people, most often having to do with speculation about surgeries we might or might not have had. There are too many rules for us and how we want to manage our bodies, too many costs—financial and emotional—that aren't covered. Too many things we "should" be or do or act like. As a trans man, I want to help feminism include trans people and all the bodies that need care and love and safety.

Feminism is about advocating for equality for all women, not just people you're comfortable with. It's about standing for people who are other than you, and amplifying their voices, instead of standing against them or speaking for them. It's about making the world better, and kinder. Your feminism can be more powerful than any generation's has ever been, if it opens itself to everyone who needs it. You can take over the world with your empathy and inclusion. And I hope you will.

Do Female Black Lives Matter Too?

BY AMANDLA STENBERG

 amandla stenberg `+FOLLOW`

BLACK FEATURES ARE BEAUTIFUL. BLACK WOMEN ARE NOT.
WHITE WOMEN ARE PARAGONS OF VIRTUE AND DESIRE.
BLACK WOMEN ARE OBJECTS OF FETISHISM AND BRUTALITY.

This, at least, **seems to be the mentality surrounding black femininity** and beauty in a society built upon **eurocentric beauty standards.** While white women are praised for altering their bodies, plumping their lips, and tanning their skin, **black women are shamed although the same features exist on them naturally.**

This double standard is one string in the netting that surrounds black female sexuality—**a web that entraps black women when they claim sexual agency.** Deeply ingrained into culture is the notion that **black female bodies, at the intersect of oppression, are less than human** and therefore unattractive. They are symbols of pain, trauma, and **degradation.** Often when they are sexualized, it is from a place of **racial fetishism.**

Black feminine sexuality is a tender spot—tender with deep-rooted suppression and taboo—**the effects of which are pervasive.**

The stigmas surrounding it are embedded in American infrastructure and psyche as evidenced by the ways black women are sexually assaulted and treated by police—acts that go frequently unreported by the media. **When the media is not ignoring black women all together, they are disparaging them.**

As culture shifts and racial tensions are tested through the vehicle of the #BlackLivesMatter movement, it is important to question:

Do female black lives matter too?

♥ **38.3K likes**   💬 **9,042 comments**

THE FOLLOWING TRANSCRIPT COMES FROM A PREVIOUSLY PUBLISHED PHOTO BY
AMANDLA STENBERG, WHICH CAN BE VIEWED AT INSTAGRAM.COM/AMANDLASTENBERG

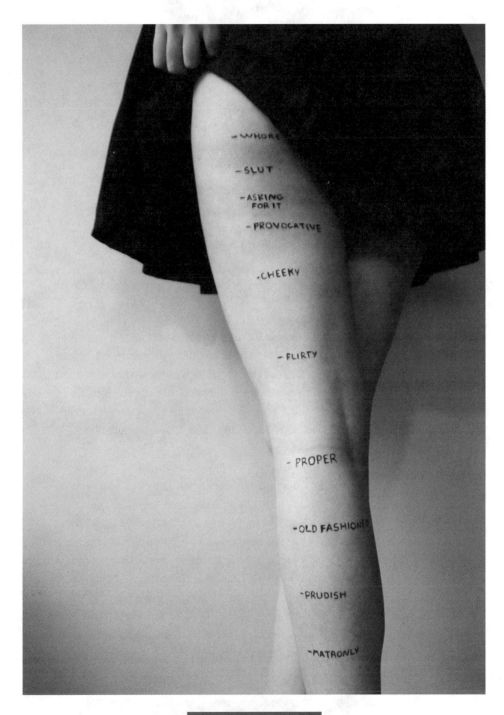

JUDGMENTS by Pomona Lake

An Interview with Laverne Cox: "I Absolutely Consider Myself a Feminist"

BY TRICIA ROMANO

In many ways, actress Laverne Cox is the perfect face for the transgender movement. The image of this first trans person ever to grace the cover of *Time* magazine makes it increasingly clear why she is a "sought-after celebrity," as the magazine described her. Beautiful and telegenic, intelligent, with a razor-sharp wit, Cox can speak eloquently about being bullied as a youth and rising above it to become who she was meant to be; she can school the uninformed on the complex issues about being trans in a way that's patient and clear, without ever being condescending. In her interview with Katie Couric, she deflected embarrassing, intrusive questions about her body parts with grace and ease.

If the trans community could create a perfect ambassador for its cause, it would be hard to top Cox. For many Americans, her character, Sophia Burset on Netflix's *Orange Is the New Black*, is the first trans woman they've ever met either in real life or on TV. In the first season, they learned about the things that many trans women struggle with via Sophia—how she needs access to hormones and without them her physical transition is in jeopardy; how her status as a woman in the world is constantly challenged and threatened; and how she risks losing the people she loves the most (her wife and son) in order to become herself.

DAME magazine's Tricia Romano spoke with Laverne about the pressures of being the spokesperson for trans women, correct gender pronouns, life before transition, and how trans women are becoming the most out-spoken feminists at a time when feminism is apparently a dirty word with young female celebrities.

Hi, Laverne! You are now probably the most famous trans woman in the world.

Oh my God.

Is that weird to think that?

It's really weird to think that. There has to be a more famous trans woman in the world. I'm sure there are.

I don't think so. Before you transitioned, would you have considered yourself a feminist? Do you consider yourself one now?

I absolutely considered myself a feminist before I transitioned. When I was in college, I was very interested in women's studies. [The writer] bell hooks was like my feminist godmother. Her book *Black Look* changed the way I thought about race and gender. I was in a sort of androgynous place, figuring out who I was. I've always been interested in feminist politics, particularly because of my mother. Growing up in Alabama, which was sort of ground zero for a lot of civil-rights struggles that we had in this country, I got politicized around race as well.

How do you think your relationship to feminism changed since you transitioned?

I think it's the lived experience of being a woman and what it means to be a woman in public space and how men relate to me. It's funny, because I feel like men relate to me in similar ways that they did before I transitioned, because I was always really feminine and I was in this androgynous place, so I almost feel like I didn't have full access to patriarchy or to male privilege. Feminism really gave us the critique of essentialized womanhood, right? In the beginning of the second wave of feminism, it was mostly a straight white woman thing. And there were a lot of lesbian feminists and a lot of black women who were, like bell hooks famously said, "Ain't I a woman?" And so feminism gave us this critique of the idea that womanhood is this disessential thing—that one is not born a woman but rather becomes one, as Simone de Beauvoir wrote in *The Second Sex*.

What do you think of this infighting between "natural born" women and trans women with the former saying that trans women can't really be feminists?

We're talking about separatist feminists—like they don't believe that trans women are women. It's a very retrograde kind of feminism where there is an essentialized idea of womanhood. I think anti-essentialist feminists have had this conversation. But the reality is that trans women are being excluded from a lot of women's spaces throughout the country because of that. I think it's really just, "Who is a woman? And are we just our bodies? Are we just our ovaries or lack thereof?" And womanhood is so much more complicated than that. And everyone's gender is so much more complicated than that. And assuming that everyone has this universal experience around privilege, too, is very problematic. You know, I was really feminine. I wore makeup and dresses before I transitioned. I probably have more privilege now since I've transitioned because I'm like more clearly delineated in some sort of more identifiable gender space than I was before I transitioned. It really, really discredits the real, lived experiences of a lot of trans women and goes to the heart of really what trans folks are fighting: the stigma that we're not who we say we are. Trans women are women.

Do you think that people are learning a lot about trans issues through your character? Do they realize how universal those themes are?

It's hard to say for sure. People are connecting with her as a human being, and they're seeing a trans woman character as a human being, played by an actual trans woman. And so when we begin to connect with people as human beings, then it becomes really difficult to discriminate against them, and to say that they don't deserve life and that they are not human beings.

Why do you think trans women tend to be better about talking about feminist issues?

I don't like making blanket statements like that, but my womanhood is something that I've had to claim. I think trans women, and trans people in general, show everyone that you can define what it means to be a man or woman on your own terms. A lot of what feminism is about is moving outside of roles and moving outside of expectations of who and what you're supposed to be to live a more authentic life.

We talked about you being now one of the most famous trans women in the world. Do you feel pressure to shed light on certain topics? What topics does the general public most need help with understanding?

Yes, I feel pressure. I think the biggest thing is taking the stigma away from being trans. And the stigma leads to criminalization. The stigma leads to violence. And that trans women are women and just using the correct pronouns to refer to us and respecting who we say we are. I've become keenly aware that when we're misgendered with the use of the wrong pronouns, that misgendering leads directly to violence against us.

Last year, I was at this vigil for Islan Nettles, this twenty-one-year-old trans woman of color who was murdered in New York City. Some of her family members and community members stood up on stage and—after the young girl had been brutally beaten on the streets of New York—used male pronouns to refer to her. There were such grimaces from people in the audience and such pain attached to that misgendering.

I'm just speculating that "You're a man, you're a dude" may have been the last thing she heard before she was murdered. And so it's so important to just respect people for who they are, and if you're not sure of what gender pronoun to use, ask. I've been saying this a lot lately: Cornel West reminds us that justice is what love looks like out in public. And I think if we have love for transgender people and love for people who are disenfranchised, that love will manifest itself in public policy and how we treat people and giving them housing, health care, employment. Trans people need a lot of love out in public, right now.

THIS PIECE WAS PREVIOUSLY PUBLISHED IN *DAME* MAGAZINE.

Feminism Is
as Feminism Does

BY MIA AND MICHAELA DEPRINCE

MIA & MICHAELA:

We spent our earliest years in Sierra Leone, one of the world's least developed countries. There, it was acceptable for men to beat their wives and daughters, deny their daughters an education, and traffic them into slavery for labor on the cacao plantations of West Africa, or in the sex trade. The treatment of women worsened during the country's civil war. What began as a revolution to protest the absence of jobs and lack of educational opportunities turned into a frenzy of anger and frustration. It erupted as a volcano of violence primarily directed at women and girls. Physicians for Human Rights estimates that between 215,000 and 257,000 of Sierra Leone's women and girls, some of them just small children, were subjected to sexual violence.

We emerged from this war at the age of four as staunch feminists, but ours was a feminism forged by anger, hatred, and fear of men. We were fortunate to be adopted by an American mother and father who were feminists—both believed that men, women, and those who identify along the gender spectrum should have equal rights and opportunities. Both parents encouraged and supported our interests and talents so that we would grow up to be strong, independent women with something to offer this world. Both taught us by example that feminism did not require us to be angry, hateful, and frightened.

While being nurtured in this equal-opportunity environment, we grew to understand feminism and realized that it cannot be solely a women's movement. It must be a human movement, supported by fathers, brothers, sons, uncles, and cousins. When we speak of feminism to women, it's like preaching to the choir. Women know that they are people. Even the most repressed woman has an innate sense of her own value. It's men who sometimes need to learn that the women in their lives are people, deserving the same rights that they themselves enjoy.

Perhaps the phrase "that they themselves enjoy" is the key to understanding why there are many places in the world where women are so beaten down. Though violence against women and subjugation of women still exist among the wealthy and highly educated, the statistics compiled by the United Nations and the World Health Organization show that these evils are most prominent in undeveloped regions of poverty, unemployment, lawlessness, and illiteracy.

A few years ago, we listened to three young Pakistani women who were interviewed at a Women in the World Summit. They were talking about the struggle to convince men to allow their daughters to go to school. One of the women said that in one village, when she promised to provide an education to the men of the village, the elders allowed the daughters to be educated as well. The men had feared that if they themselves remained uneducated, the women would show disdain toward them, or leave them behind. But that was only one tiny village with a handful of elders. The problem extends across most of the globe, especially in Sub-Sahara Africa. So how do we reach millions, or possibly even billions of people, who are entrenched in misogynist behavior? We cannot possibly educate and feed all the men of the world so that their wives, too, can learn and eat. So what can we do to help?

Here is where my sister and I part ways. Though we are both making an effort to spread feminism throughout the world, we go about it differently. We each have chosen a different cause to champion.

MICHAELA:

For many, many years, I wanted to be a ballerina. Nothing but ballet interested me. As a child, I imagined myself on the magnificent stages of the world, wearing luscious tutus, doing pirouettes, grand jetés, and fouetté turns on elaborately designed stages. As a child, I believed this was all there was to the life of a ballerina, and I felt that it was enough for me. And if I were Russian, French, or from any other European nation, it might have been enough, and probably all anyone would have expected from me was that I be a great ballet dancer.

But I am an African ballerina. After I appeared in the documentary film *First Position*, I was thrust into the public eye, and as time went on, much more than good dancing was expected of me. When I opened the 2013 Women in the World Summit in NYC, so many people assumed that I had the power to inspire and influence.

My mother, whom you may know from the books we have coauthored, has had the most profound effect on my life. She told me that because of my celebrity, I had been granted the power to affect lives—and that I must not waste it. So now, I have decided to use that power to help change the lives of women in my native country, as well as the lives of women in other parts the world, from countries in Africa, Asia, the Middle East, and in pockets of Europe and North America, where people have migrated.

I know that the world is in need of many changes, but the particular cause I've chosen involves what I believe to be the greatest human rights violation perpetuated collectively upon women, and one of the most brutal manifestations of gender inequality. I have chosen to advocate for a worldwide ban on the mutilation or cutting of female genitals, also known as FGM. I cannot begin to convince men to love and recognize the value of their women if women cannot love themselves. And in my eyes, FGM is a violation perpetuated upon women by other women, and proof of self-loathing.

In most cultures where it is practiced, FGM is considered a rite of passage, preparing girls for their future as wives. It is traditionally believed to excise the male parts of a woman's body, the parts that allow women to experience pleasure during sexual intercourse. It is believed to leave the girl pure and clean, devoid of the ability to enjoy sex. Women in societies that practice FGM believe that the ritual makes them more feminine and thus more attractive to men. A social study established that FGM raises the social status for the family and generates income when the daughter marries and the dowry is paid.

The World Health Organization and UNICEF define FGM as any procedures involving partial or total removal of the external female genitalia or other injury to the female genital organs for nonmedical reasons. It results in the spread of infection, including HIV, through the use of unclean instruments, loss of blood that can result in shock and death, pain, trauma, maternal death in childbirth, infant mortality, and a lifetime of painful sex.

Before and during the civil war in Sierra Leone, the rate of FGM was estimated at 95 percent. As a female child born in Sierra Leone, I should have fallen victim to this practice. Ironically, it is probably vitiligo, the skin condition that left me spotted, and subject to harassment and abuse, that protected me. Since I wasn't considered marriageable anyway, my uncle would not have wasted his money paying for this procedure. But some of the other young girls who ended up living in my orphanage experienced FGM.

Now the rate is 88 percent, and though FGM is still not illegal in Sierra Leone, laws have been passed to limit the legal age of this barbaric procedure to eighteen and above. Unfortunately, these laws are ineffective because Sierra Leone does not have the ability to police their violation, so children are still cut and perpetrators are not prosecuted. It is not ethics or respect for the rights of women that has lowered the incidence of FGM. It's the fear of the spread of Ebola. When the fear subsides, will the rate increase again?

FGM is not limited to Sierra Leone. Over 133 million girls and women in twenty-nine countries in Africa and the Middle East have experienced FGM. Migrant families from these countries, who now live in the UK, the United States, and other countries, often bring their daughters for summer vacations in their native lands. The summer vacation is really an opportunity for their daughters to be mutilated.

For these reasons, I want to use my influence as a well-known African ballerina to spread a message of feminism. The practice of FGM does not speak of equal rights and opportunities for women. But like the three Pakistani girls, I have to give the men a reason to become involved. Perhaps the message they need to hear is that wives who have not been cut will be healthier, survive childbirth, and live to raise healthy children. They might also benefit from learning that an uncut woman will welcome their overtures of love, not just endure them, thus strengthening their marriage. We don't have the answer yet, but we know it's not keeping men out. We want men to understand this issue and to ask them to play a key role in creating a solution. Let us invite men to become feminists along with their wives, daughters, mothers, and sisters.

MIA:

During the civil war in Sierra Leone, rebels fought for the control of the alluvial diamond mines. They did not use these diamonds to provide food, shelter, medical care, and education to the people. Perhaps if they had, there would have been adequate doctors and hospitals to stop the recent Ebola epidemic. But no, the rebels used the diamonds—blood diamonds—to purchase powerful weapons. I have often wondered why, if the rebels had such powerful weapons at their disposal, they had to resort to the use of their penises as weapons against the women and girls in Sierra Leone.

Dr. Olabisi Cole works at the International Rescue Committee's Rainbow Centers in Freetown and Kenema, Sierra Leone, providing medical care for girls and women who have been victims of sexual violence. Dr. Cole lived in Sierra Leone during the civil war. She observed how rape and violence became part of the mainstream culture during that period. It was a habit, a learned behavior, as difficult to overcome, or even more so, than the drug habits they picked up while in the service of the rebels. According to Dr. Cole, as young men, those who learned as child soldiers to rape during the civil war, now use sexual violence gratuitously or as a tool to get their way. Sierra Leone is not an isolated case. There were twenty thousand to eighty thousand rapes in Nanjing, China, in 1937; two hundred thousand rapes in Bangladesh in 1971; forty thousand rapes in Bosnia-Herzegovina from 1991 to 1994; five hundred thousand rapes in Rwanda in 1994; and more than a thousand rapes occur every day in the Democratic Republic of Congo and the Sudan.

In May 2011, seven women, all Nobel Laureates, met with a group of over one hundred powerful women from around the world to develop strategies to stop the use of rape as a weapon in conflict situations. They concluded that a resolution to this problem requires the commitment of not only women, but also of men who respect and care about women. This is an issue that needs the intervention of political leadership on an international level to prevent, protect, and prosecute in order to stop rape in conflict. Prevent, protect, prosecute—these three key words are fundamental to the goal of "the International Campaign to Stop Rape and Gender Violence in Conflict."

I believe that prevention is the most powerful of these tools. Stop it before it happens through education and conditioning against rape. Women certainly know what they have lost through rape, but do the men? Do the rebels who rampaged through Sierra Leone, raping and terrorizing, recognize what their actions have cost their sons? Do they understand that the young men of their country have lost their moral compass? The men of that country—of any country—need to learn what Dr. Cole has discovered.

I am not a celebrity like my sister, Michaela. I'm an emerging singer/songwriter and instrumentalist still working on my college degree. But even I can contribute to this cause. One of the first things I have done is to turn my back on all music that fosters violence against women in its lyrics, and publicly speak out against it.

In 2001, the *Journal of Criminal Justice and Popular Culture* published a report by Edward G. Armstrong of Murray State University on the topic of misogyny in gangsta rap. Armstrong concludes that gangsta rap music continues to teach, promote, and glamorize violence and misogyny. He cites research that confirms that listening to gangsta rap music motivates sexual aggression and inappropriate behavior, and its lyrics significantly increase men's adversarial sexual beliefs. If this can happen in a country like the United States, with compulsory education and an intact justice system with the power to prosecute acts of sexual violence, imagine the effect that gangsta rap has on the young men in a country ravaged by conflict!

Even now, while my career is in its early stages, I use the power of the pen, the keys of my piano, and the strings of my guitar not only to send the message to women that they should embrace feminism, but to teach the men and boys whom they love to embrace it as well by advocating on behalf of women against violence and rape at home as well as in conflict.

In 2013, my mother brought me to the Women in the World Summit in New York City. One evening, after all the speeches and interviews at the summit, I joined the crowds of women as we piled into cars and drove to the United Nations for the Diane von Furstenberg Awards. There I met Diane von Furstenberg and Gloria Steinem. Now I participate in this event annually—not for the celebrities I meet, but for the courage and commitment it brings out in me. It was this summit that inspired me to write and compose a song aptly titled "Women in the World."

I sing thank you to the mammas Truth,
Steinem and Friedan,
Who said woman's more than Adam's
rib, turning views around.

I sing of courage to the women, who
march arm in arm,
Risking hate, risking their jobs, risking
ridicule and harm.

I sing power to the daughters that
watched their mothers cry,
Who challenge ignorant tyranny,
unafraid to die.

Chorus:
But it's not enough
Because the job is tough,
And we'll never end our fight
Until the whole world sees the light
Of the Women in the World.

I sing praise to young women from
Michaela to Malala,
Who won't accept bigotry, and say
time for change is now.

I sing power to the little girls, who
want to change their plight,
Who yearn to go to school and learn,
and feel they have that right.

I sing thank you to the mammas, with
strong arms opened wide,
As they reach out to the orphans, and
draw them to their side.

Chorus:
But it's not enough
Because the job is tough,
And we'll never end our fight
Until the whole world sees the light
Of the Women in the World.

I sing praise to the women, of both
poverty and note,
Who breach barriers of custom, to
help their sisters vote.

I sing thank you to the women of
invention and design,
With ideas and ambitions, our lives
they redefine.

I sing power to the mammas, who
teach their tiny boys,
The value of their sisters, who are
neither slaves nor toys.

Chorus:
But it's not enough
Because the job is tough,
And we'll never end our fight
Until the whole world sees the light
Of the Women in the World.

Oh yes, Oh-oh yes, I do declare . . .

But it's not enough
Because the job is tough,
And we'll never end our fight
Until the whole world sees the light
Of the Women in the World.

Of the Women in the World,
Oh yes, Oh-oh yes, of the Women in
the World

MIA & MICHAELA:

When we were barely into our teens, our mother told us an interesting fact about being a teenager in the early 1960s. She said that in those prefeminist years, before Gloria Steinem was nationally recognized as a leader and spokeswoman for the feminist movement, and before Betty Friedan's famous book, *The Feminine Mystique*, was released, engulfing the country in a new wave of feminism, quaint courtship customs existed. One of them involved boys asking their girlfriends to prove their love. Of course, as you might imagine, this required the girl to surrender her virginity to the boy. Quite often, in those prefeminist times, the boy then felt culturally influenced to lose respect for his girlfriend and compelled to brag about his conquest to his friends. Though this thinking hasn't completely died, advocates of feminism have empowered young women to speak out, make choices, and extend ultimatums.

Now here's an appropriate reversal. Ask the young man in your life to prove his love for you twenty-first-century style, by embracing feminism. After all, feminism is no more than advocating for equal rights and opportunities for women everywhere . . . all women everywhere, no matter their race, religion, disability, or sexual orientation. If he loves you, then he will respect you, and what more perfect way is there for him to demonstrate that love and respect than by supporting your advocacy on behalf of feminism?

Young women, do not be afraid to label yourself a feminist, because it is definitely not a synonym for misandrist—man hater. Feminist is not a label for lesbian; it is not a label for straight—gay and straight, bi, trans, queer, and gender-nonconforming people can all be feminists. Feminists include thinkers and doers, laborers and professionals, athletes and artists, paupers and presidents. The problems of subjugated and abused women are so great that the cause needs everyone. The best way we can describe it is, "Feminism Is as Feminism Does."

RESOURCES/FURTHER READING:

- Rape Is Civil War's Legacy in Sierra Leone, PBS, October 1, 2012: http://video.pbs.org/video/2258504182/.

- Simpson, Deanna, "Women under Siege—Conflict Profiles," February 7, 2013: http://www.womenundersiegeproject.org /conflicts/profile/sierra-leone.

- *We'll Kill You If You Cry: Sexual Violence in the Sierra Leone Conflict*, Human Rights Watch, January 16, 2003: https://www.hrw.org/report /2003/01/16/well-kill-you-if-you-cry/sexual-violence-sierra-leone -conflict.

- *Women Forging a New Security: Ending Sexual Violence in Conflict*, Conference Report 2011, January 10, 2012: http:// nobelwomensinitiative.org/2012/01/conference-report-women -forging-a-new-security-ending-sexual-violence-in-conflict/.

- "Consequences of FGM" from African Women: http://www.african -women.org/FGM/consequences.php.

- "Female Genital Mutilation/Cutting: Data and Trends Update 2010" from the Population Reference Bureau: http://www.prb.org /Publications/Datasheets/2010/fgm2010.

- "Female Genital Mutilation" from the United Nations Population Fund: http://www.unfpa.org/female-genital-mutilation.

- "Health Complications of Female Genital Mutilation," from the World Health Organization: http://www.who.int/reproductivehealth /topics/fgm/health_consequences_fgm/en/.

- O'Carroll, Lisa, *Guardian*, "Sierra Leone's Secret FGM Societies spread silent fear and sleepless nights," August 24, 2015: http:// www.theguardian.com/global-development/2015/aug/24/sierra -leone-female-genital-mutilation-soweis-secret-societies-fear.

CULTURE

AND

POP

CULTURE

CHAPTER four

ON the MTV MUSIC AWARDS STAGE

in 2014, Beyoncé performed in front
of a large screen proclaiming
"Feminist."

Celebrities like Taylor Swift have come to embrace the label—and, thanks to the help of wise women in her life like Nicki Minaj, she understands how broad and important intersectional feminism is. Still, other celebrities, like Shailene Woodley, eschew the label, often with the misunderstanding that "feminism" means "hating men."

Beyond popular culture, though, are the broader questions about feminism: Who is allowed to adopt feminism and where are people allowed to be feminists? How does feminism intersect with race or religion or history? "Are you a feminist?" and "Can you be a feminist if _____?" are two questions budding and seasoned feminists hear again and again because the concept is so multidimensional. These questions come from a place of both fascination and confusion.

Let's take a peek at the ways feminism affects culture on all levels.

Somewhere in America

BY ZARIYA ALLEN

here in america, in every single state,
they have a set of standards, for every subject—
a collection of lessons that the teacher is required to teach by the end
of the term
but the greatest lessons you will ever teach us will not come from your
syllabus.

**The greatest lessons you will ever teach us you will not even
remember.**

you never told us what we weren't allowed to say
we just learned how to hold our tongues

**Now somewhere in America there is a child holding a copy of
The Catcher in the Rye and there is a child holding a gun.**

but only one of these things has been banned by their state government
and it's not the one that can rip through flesh

it's the one that says "Fuck you" on more pages than one

because we must control what the people say
how they think
and if they wanna become the overseer of their own selves

then we'll show them a real one

somewhere in america
there is a child sitting at his mother's computer
reading the home page
of the KKK's website,
and that's open to the public
but that child will have never read *To Kill a Mockingbird*
because his school has banned it for its use of the N-word

maya angelou is prohibited because we're not allowed to talk about
    rape in school

we were taught that just because something happens
doesn't mean you are to talk about it

they build us brand-new shopping malls
so that you'll forget where we're really standing:
on the bones of the hispanics
on the bones of the slaves
on the bones of the native americans
on the bones of those who fought just to speak

transcontinental railroad to japanese internment camps
There are things missing from our history books.
But we were taught that it is better to be silent
than to make them uncomfortable.

somewhere in america
private school girls search for hours through boutiques
trying to find the prom dress of their dreams
while kids on the south side spend hours searching through the lost
    and found
cause winter's coming soon
and that's the only jacket they have

kids are late to class for working the midnight shift

they give awards for best attendance but not keeping your family
     off the streets

these kids will call your music ghetto
they will tell you you don't talk right
then they'll get in the backseat of a car with all their friends
singin 'bout how they're
'bout that life, and we can't stop

Somewhere in America schools are promoting self confidence
while they whip out their scales and shout out your body fat percentage
     in class.
Where the heftier girls are hiding away
and the slim fit beauties can't help but giggle with pride.

the preppy kids go thrift shopping cause they think it sounds real hip
     and real fun
but we go cause that's all we've got money for,
cause momma works for the city
momma only gets paid once a month

SOMEWHERE IN AMERICA
a girl's getting felt up by a grown man on the subway
she's still in her school uniform and that's part of the appeal

it's hard to run in knee socks and mary janes
and all her male teachers know it, too

coaches cover up their star players raping freshmen after the dance
young women are killed for rejecting dates
but god forbid i bring my girlfriend to prom

a girl's black out drunk at the after party
take a picture before her wounds wake her

how many pixels is your sanity worth
what's a 4.0 to a cold jury

what'd you learn in class today?
Don't walk fast
don't speak loud
keep your hands to yourself
keep your head down
keep your eyes on your own paper
if you don't know the answer, fill in c
always wear earbuds when you ride the bus alone
if you feel like someone is following you, **pretend you're on the phone**
a teacher never fails
only you do

EVERY STATE IN AMERICA

the greatest lessons
are the ones you don't remember learning

Choose Your Own Adventure: Why Fandom Is Right for You (Yes, You!)

BY BRENNA CLARKE GRAY

Do you ever watch a movie and think, *Man, I love everything about this except how that one woman gets treated?* Do you read novels and wish two characters would hook up, but they never do? Do you love to geek out and argue about the really nitty-gritty details of the stuff you like? Then fandom is most definitely for you: It's a place where you can take those characters you love and reinvent their situations, bend their race and gender, and experiment with their sexuality. It's a space that treats fiction as fluid and puts you in control of how the story gets told. And most important, it's dominated by girls just like you.

What is fandom?

Fandom comes from the word "fan," and at its core it's about liking something—a lot. But the difference between just being a fan of something and belonging to a fandom is best summed up in one word: "commitment." A fan might enjoy the Harry Potter series and might own a T-shirt and all the books and films. Someone who considers themselves a member of the fandom, however, will do all of that, but might also write their own stories or create their own art about the characters and spend lots of time on Tumblr talking to other people who do the same. Fan art and fan fiction (or fanfic) are the lifeblood of fandom. Imagine taking the characters you love and remixing their adventures to tell a completely different story about their experiences: make a character break up with a lover you don't like; kill off a villain you're tired of; explore what these characters would be like if they had different races, gender expressions, or sexuality. When you commit to a fandom, you're committing to a whole new way of looking at the media you love, and you're taking possession of it in a way that many young women find exciting, empowering, and unlike anything they've experienced before.

There are fandoms for everything from bands to politicians, but the most common fandoms are for books, television shows, and movies. The history of fandom goes back a long way, because people have always loved stories and retelling stories in their own way. Some people argue that Jane Austen was the first figure who inspired fandom. Others say Sherlock Holmes fans were the first example of a modern fandom because, way back in the Victorian period, they organized themselves to convince Sir Arthur Conan Doyle to keep writing Sherlock Holmes stories, even though he really wanted to stop (and we can even find examples of Sherlock Holmes fanfic from 1897!).

Wait a minute. I've heard about fanfic. Isn't it ...dirty?

No. And yes! Both no and yes. And that's what makes fan fiction so great.

So you might have heard about fan fiction in terms of something called "slash," which people sometimes talk about while giggling behind their hands. Slash is definitely a big part of many fandoms and refers to creating stories that discuss the sexual relationships between two characters—usually of the same sex—that don't exist in the original texts or canon. (Fans call the novel or show or film made by the original creators the "canon." Fandom-originated ideas that everyone agrees with are "fanon," and ideas about the characters that are true only to you are called your "head canon." So fanfic is about changing the canon to align with your head canon, and hoping that the community likes it so much, it becomes fanon. Get it?) Slash is a pretty widespread phenomenon in fandom.

Slash fiction seems to have emerged as part of the *Star Trek* fandom. Women have always had an important presence in fan culture, and it's women fans who created the concept of slash. The story goes that women who watched *Star Trek* wanted to read erotic stories about Kirk and Spock, but they didn't want to read about these characters—whom they had massive crushes on!—being with other women. So they created stories about romantic liaisons between Kirk and Spock, or Kirk/Spock stories, and the punctuation gave its name to a whole genre of storytelling for fans that remains dominated by female storytellers. And in spite of the heteronormative origins of this very public and queer mode of remixing the canon, it's worth noting that lots of people read slash fiction because they can see themselves in the stories in a way they usually don't get to in mainstream media.

Most slash fiction tells erotic stories about men. This probably has a lot to do with the average cast of movie or TV show: there are a lot of dudes on our television sets and in our multiplexes, ladies. Think about a typical cast of main characters in a Marvel movie: men way outnumber women! So if you're remixing those characters in romantic fanfic, there are a lot more possibilities if you let the men couple up, too. This is an important way that fandom changes the dominant narrative in the media we consume. Instead of all the stories being about heterosexual romance, slash turns the tables by making homosexuality the norm within its context. This is one space where we assume characters will be gay unless the author tells us otherwise, which is pretty different than what we're used to seeing.

But it's important to note that slash is only one subset of the world of fan fiction. Lots of fanfic is just about remixing situations. For example, what if Harry and Hermione dated? What if Draco and Ron were best friends? How would the universe you love change if some key element was different? And part of this connects to the explicitly feminist nature of fandom: you can write anything. If you think Luke Skywalker should have been black, you can write that story. If you want Captain America to be a woman, you can write that story. If you wonder what would change if Katniss were asexual, you can write that story. And in all of these cases, if you're not really one for writing, you can create in other ways: write a song about why Black Widow needs more airtime, or paint a picture of Spiderman as a Latino teenager.

This all fits into a larger kind of storytelling sometimes called race or gender or sexuality "bending," and it is an important way in which fandom helps people feel more included. Fandom takes the holes in representation of all kinds of groups in mainstream media and rights (and rewrites!) those wrongs. This is the empowering magic of fandom. If you're tired of not seeing the real world represented in the art you love, go see what your fellow fans have been doing. You'll be inspired and amazed.

You say fandom is feminist, but I always hear people talk about "fanboys." Isn't this a guy thing?

No! This is probably the biggest misconception about fandom. For some reason, we think that only boys want to geek out and get really excited about their favorite things. Maybe our minds go to a (not very accurate) stereotype we have of Sci-Fi conventions or video gamers. We're used to seeing the typical media representation of a nerd being a straight white guy. Boring, you guys. Because women are *everywhere* in fandom; indeed, in many fandoms, the majority of active, engaged fans are young women. In fact, women dominate on Tumblr, which is the primary place young fans congregate online, and women and men under thirty actually attend conventions in equal numbers now. More and more conventions are including feminist tracks to give you a dedicated space to talk about geek girl culture. If a convention you want to attend doesn't have a place to talk about this stuff, you should ask for one—or better yet, offer to organize it! So a guy thing? No way.

And don't you go thinking this is some new thing, either. Women have always been an important part of fandom and were in on the ground floor with starting *Star Trek* conventions and fanzines. *Star Trek* was a show that prioritized diversity and inclusion, and its fandom did the same. In fact, three women—Jacqueline Lichtenberg, Sondra Marshak, and Joan Winston— wrote *Star Trek Lives!* in 1975 about the fandom of *Star Trek*. This book is considered a seminal record of the fandom, but it also is credited with giving far more people access to the *Star Trek* fandom than had been possible before. Remember, in 1975 there was no Internet, so finding this book at a store or a library, if you were a fan, too, would have been a lifeline to a whole community of people just like you. And when we consider that *Star Trek* really set the model for all the media fandoms that would come later, we see the true impact of women in fandom. So don't let anyone call you a "fake geek girl" or ask you to prove your knowledge about the media you love before you get to participate. You have nothing to prove. Young women just like you are an essential part of the DNA of fandom.

How do I get involved? And why should I?

The great thing about this moment in history is that it has never been easier to find other people who like the same stuff that you like. Once upon a time, if you liked, say, *Star Trek*, you would have to come across a copy of *Star Trek Lives!* or be tipped off to a fanzine from someone in the know. You would subscribe, write in to the fanzine looking for other people to connect with, and then you could exchange letters via snail mail. You might decide to go to a convention to meet other fans, or you might even organize a gathering yourself. It took a lot of work to get into fandom, and you really had to commit before you even knew if it was a good fit for you.

Now, every fandom is accessible right at your fingertips. Many fans use Tumblr to post their fanart and talk about their fandom, but lots of fandoms have their own websites as well, usually with discussion forums, so Google is a good friend here. Once you find somewhere to check out, spend some time getting to know the community before you start posting. We call this lurking, and it's a good way to get a feel of whether the community is something you want to engage with. You might ask yourself whether this place feels welcoming to you: Do people seem to argue in a civil way? Are you comfortable with the kinds of language and images people use to express themselves? Are young women and people of color contributing to the conversation? The great thing about fandom online is that there are lots of different groups and communities for each book, movie, or TV show you love, so shop around. Find a place that makes you feel safe and able to discuss your ideas openly and freely.

Once you've found a place, remember that the best part of fandom is expressing yourself. You can start small, by posting a review of an episode of a TV show or responding to someone's gif post to thank them for making the images. Or you can jump in with both feet and try writing some fanfic, making a video blog, recording a song you wrote about the show, or posting a picture you've created of the main characters. Fandom is by nature creative and collaborative, so people might give you ideas to improve your art, and they'll definitely give you lots of encouragement. Make sure you engage with the community and share your work—it's okay to ask people to read your stories or listen to your songs, and be ready to embrace their work, too. Fandom works because people want to read and share not just their work, but the work of fellow fans, too.

And did you know fandoms can change the world, in ways big and small? For example, when fans organize, they have the power to save cancelled shows—*Star Trek* and *Community* are just two examples—or bring back favorite shows as movies. *Firefly* became the film *Serenity*, and *Veronica Mars* fans rallied to crowd-fund its movie. But fandoms are also often connected with important charity projects; the Harry Potter Alliance or John and Hank Green's Nerdfighters are probably the best-known recent examples, having between them raised millions of dollars and encouraged volunteerism for projects all over the world. When people group together out of love, they can do really exciting things!

So, to wrap this all up . . .

You know, sometimes we can get pretty down about the lack of representation of women, queer identities, and people of color in the contemporary media landscape. Things are definitely changing for the better, but the world of television and film and bestselling YA fiction can all feel very white, and very straight, and very male. If those experiences don't reflect your experiences, it can be really alienating. While it's not a replacement for Hollywood getting its act together, fandom can inspire and empower you to think about the world in different ways and to create a universe for characters you love that you can tailor to look a lot more like you. Like anything online, you should be safe—use a pseudonym, lurk to understand the community fully, and don't post anything private or that makes you uncomfortable. But when you find a place where you feel safe to discuss your ideas, your relationship to media will change in really interesting ways.

Get out there and get consuming and creating fan-created content. Make the world you want to live in. Choose your own adventure. And have fun!

DRAWING FOR INSPIRATION by Michelle Hiraishi

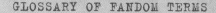

GLOSSARY OF FANDOM TERMS

Here are a few words and phrases you might come across
as you engage in fandom, and what they mean.

- **BETA:** When you get involved in the community, someone might ask you to beta their writing. This means reading and editing it for clarity and coherence before the larger audience gets access to it. Really great betas (or beta-readers) are in hot demand, so if you're more into polishing than creating, this can be a great role to play.

- **COSPLAY:** Dressing up like your favorite characters. This is really common at conventions (or cons), but more clothing lines are offering options for everyday cosplay, like a cardigan that looks suspiciously like Superman's cape, for example.

- **CROSSOVER:** Fandoms like to cross-pollinate like crazy, so sometimes you'll see fandoms overlapping and creating fiction from multiple worlds at once. Dr. Who and Sherlock fandoms often overlap, and SuperWhoLock adds the Supernatural fandom to the mix to create a massively popular crossover grouping.

- **FANZINES:** Self-published paper magazines featuring fanfiction and fan news, and even in our seemingly all-digital world, they still exist today.

- **FILK AND NERDCORE:** Two kinds of music written and performed by fans. The content of both is any kind of nerdy, fannish content. Filk tends stylistically to be more like folk or singer-songwriter music, whereas nerdcore is hip-hop or rap.

- **MARY SUE/GARY STU:** An idealized protagonist in fanfic, not a character from the original canon but one created by the writer. It's usually a stand-in for the author her- or himself, and it's not a term used as a compliment.

- **SHIP:** Short for relationship, your ship is the two characters you wish would get together. Like, if you write Harry Potter fanfic and you write about Harry and Hermione getting together, you're a Harry and Hermione shipper. If that's all you ever write about, then Harry and Hermione are your OTP—one true pair.

FAQs ABOUT FEMINISM

Is it okay to call myself a feminist if I like [_____]?

Feminism isn't about liking only certain things or permitting yourself to enjoy only things that pose absolutely no problems. The truth is, we're all imperfect and we'll all make mistakes and do embarrassing things or act in ways that go against our feminist beliefs. What matters is that we're able to acknowledge that not all messages are great. If you love music or movies or television where, for example, women are harmed or hurt but you're okay with it, then you are absolutely still a feminist.

Many times, it's from these problematic representations that great feminist dialogue emerges. For example, fans of the long-running show *Supernatural* regularly talk about how women and people of color in the show don't have hope when they're on-screen. But this allows fans to bond over the problem while acknowledging it and begging creators to make changes that better the stories for these characters.

Facets of Feminism

BY MIKKI KENDALL

My feminism is rooted in the women who raised me and the celebrities and historical figures I looked up to as a kid. Strong women who, even if they never explicitly called themselves feminists, certainly worked toward racial and gender equality. Josephine Baker, Queen Latifah, Ida B. Wells-Barnett, and so many other strong women influenced my approach to feminism. They taught me that working toward equality meant taking as many roads as were available, and forging new ones whenever necessary. My grandmothers, aunts, and teachers made it clear that my race and my gender weren't things to choose between; they were both part of me. I learned early that working for equality and working for freedom weren't separate missions; they were part of the same hard, necessary work that we all have to do.

There's a common assumption that there is one true way to be a feminist—that there's a perfect book that will show you the right way to think, feel, and dress so that you can live up to some impossible standard. Yes, there are writers who have a lot to say about feminism, and there are certainly texts that will teach you a lot about theories like choice feminism, intersectionality, and what it means to be inclusive. But you won't and can't just learn those ideas in books or from people who call themselves feminists. You also learn those ideas from celebrities, your family members, your teachers, and from your friends.

Feminism is for all women, which means it is made up of as many approaches as there are women. You can't assume that the ideas espoused by one aspect of the feminist movement apply to every woman, much less that labeling dictates what is and is not a feminist issue. An integral part of making feminism better is to challenge yourself, the texts, and other feminists to really look at what the movement has done, or is doing to make it benefit the cause of equality and justice for *all* women.

There's no issue that impacts women that isn't a feminist issue. So whether you care about police brutality, child care, educational access, medical issues, dress codes, or something else entirely—if it's a feminist issue and if it is important to you? Then it's important to feminism. And if it isn't important to the feminists you know, or isn't a part of the texts that you have read, then you have to challenge those narratives.

Take this example: For low-income women of color, the right to work was never in doubt. They always had to work. Access to the social safety nets like welfare that were created for poor white mothers was incredibly important for the good of their children, but black women had to fight for that access. Yet, once welfare was something they could use, the narratives around it shifted to calling these black women "Welfare Queens," as though only white women's motherhood were worth protecting. While middle-class white feminists were focusing on being able to leave the home, low-income women of color were fighting to have the funds to stay at home with their children. In any narrative about the way feminism truly functions, you should expect to see people with different needs working toward different goals. There's only a problem when the more powerful groups inside feminism work against those with less power.

Feminism isn't a "get out of internalized bigotry" card. You can be a feminist and still be racist, transphobic, classist, or homophobic. You can be a feminist and still do things that harm women. Not every act or decision made by a woman will be a feminist one. Often the things that influence our expressions of feminism are rooted in our own communities and in our own biases. When talk of reproductive justice by white feminists focuses on abortion access and ignores the way the right to reproduce has throughout history been taken from communities of color, from disabled women, or from anyone who doesn't fit a narrow mold, it's not just ignorance at play. It's the very real problem of being immersed in a culture that positions motherhood as something only certain women should be able to access and protect. Yes, the right to choose when to become a parent is important; so, too, is the right to choose to stay a parent.

Every woman, cis or trans, experiences gender inequality, discrimination, or violence, but the ways they experience it differ because of factors like race, class, disability, and gender presentation. One of the most common criticisms of the mainstream feminism movement is that it centers the safety and comfort of middle-class and upper-class white women. Consider, for example, that when celebrities like Katy Perry or Miley Cyrus perform in sexually suggestive costumes, they are more likely to be hailed for their sexual empowerment by the feminist media than blasted for being bad role models. Yet, black celebrities like Beyoncé and Nicki Minaj are constantly criticized for being too sexual.

When Rihanna is criticized for wearing a sheer dress—in a nod to Josephine Baker—because somehow that isn't feminist enough for some white feminist outlets, young black girls see an accomplished black woman who isn't ashamed of her body. Who is confident in her own unique beauty. Who is showing respect to another black woman who paved the way for her to be successful. Rihanna's outfit might not seem feminist to someone not from a community that is often excluded from imagery of success or beauty, but her feminism doesn't need to speak to everyone. It needs to speak to those young girls and women who might not otherwise see themselves represented in the mainstream media.

It's racism—a product of institutional bigotry—that insists that blackness is ugly, that black women's sexuality is inherently vulgar in ways that white women's bodies are not.

It's not just celebrities who are judged by flawed feminist ideals. You can read any text from the first or second wave of feminism and find problematic narratives around gender, race, and class. Although the texts and the feminists who wrote them had good ideas that contributed to the larger goal of gender equality, their work should not be accepted uncritically. Alice Walker, for example, spoke about womanism as a direct response to the ways mainstream feminism ignored race and racism within the movement. When the movement excluded the concerns of women like her, she challenged it to expand or be left behind in favor of the next step for black women on their road to equality. Feminism isn't a glass slipper that fits only one perfect woman; it is an umbrella that has to become big enough to protect us all, even from one another.

Erasure is not equality. A feminism that is exclusionary, that makes objects out of some women and saviors out of others, is implicitly harmful. For young women of color, being able to look up to Beyoncé, Rihanna, Nicki Minaj, Laverne Cox, Janet Mock, Carmen Carrera, Lucy Liu, and others is incredibly important. People who cannot see themselves reflected in the media are people who feel like they don't have a right to speak, they don't have a right to exist, and they can't be happy. We cannot espouse ideologies that contribute to harming communities and call them feminist if we want to have feminism be for the good of all women.

An inclusive feminism is a more effective feminism.

Feminism is about action. So when we talk about feminism as a broad movement, we must remember that every community is different. The type of feminist action that one community needs may not be effective for another community. You don't have to like someone else's feminism. They may not like yours. Equality for all has never meant that everyone would agree on the best way to do anything. Understanding that what helps one community may not greatly help another is necessary for feminism to work. Race, gender, class, sexual orientation, religion, and so many other things that make every one of us unique will matter.

When Beyoncé claims the title "feminist" and shows it by supporting women by hiring them, by funding domestic violence shelters for them, but not by changing her clothes to suit an arbitrary standard, she's using her platform to carve out a place in the movement. People may lament Rihanna's refusal to let others dictate her attire, her relationship choices, or the content of her work, but she's creating a space for imperfect survivors to flourish and be complete, complex human beings in their own right. Nicki Minaj encourages girls to do well in school and to embrace their sexuality. She's also not shy about letting white women like Taylor Swift and Miley Cyrus know that their issues and challenges aren't the only ones that matter.

Marginalized women don't need other people to speak for them. They need access to the mic to speak for themselves. If you don't see someone that looks like you in mainstream feminism, you can—and should—absolutely speak up for yourself or encourage others to speak up. Find your own feminism.

OPPORTUNITY by Risa Rodil

The ONLY thing THAT separates WOMEN OF COLOR from anyone else IS OPPORTUNITY

-VIOLA DAVIS-

TOP 10 LIST OF BLACK FEMALE FRIENDS

by Brandy Colbert

1. **TLC (Tionne "T-Boz" Watkins, Rozonda "Chilli" Thomas, and Lisa "Left Eye" Lopes)**

   The bestselling American girl group of all time, TLC incorporated themes of sex positivity, self-love, and independence into their endlessly catchy R&B songs of the 1990s and 2000s. After the sudden death of Lopes, the group carried on as a duo and has said, "There will never be a replacement for Lisa."

2. **Nicole Byer and Sasheer Zamata**

   Funny ladies Byer and Zamata met through an improv team and later went on to perform at the famed Upright Citizens Brigade. While they've since branched out to separate projects (Byer on MTV's *Girl Code* and Zamata on *Saturday Night Live*), they also cocreated a Web series, *Pursuit of Sexiness*, in which they star as besties.

3. **Lisa Bonet and Cree Summer**

   Bonet and Summer starred in the groundbreaking 1980s/1990s sitcom *A Different World* and became lifelong best friends. Bonet has said, "It seems we know how to take care of each other better than we know how to take care of ourselves," while Summer affirms that "we fell instantly in love and started a very productive, creative friendship."

4. **Venus Williams and Serena Williams**

   Just a year apart in age, the Williams sisters have been playing tennis together since their days growing up in Compton, California, and competing against each other professionally since they were teenagers. While their rivalry is well-known, they share a close friendship. In 2012, they each earned their fourth Olympic gold medal, the most of any tennis player at the time.

5. **Amandla Stenberg and Willow Smith**
   Stenberg and Smith's BFF status is well documented across social media, and Stenberg has said they became friends after they began having dreams about each other. Both strongly advocate for black girls and women through activism and the clear message of staying true to yourself.

6. **Beyoncé Knowles and Kelly Rowland**
   Knowles and Rowland met when they were just children in Houston, both joining a girls group that was a precursor to the successful Destiny's Child. Rowland lived with Knowles's family for some time growing up, and the two have remained close through their years of fame, still referring to each other as sisters.

7. **Oprah Winfrey and Gayle King**
   Perhaps the most famous besties of all time, Winfrey and King met when they were working at a TV station in Baltimore and have been inseparable for more than three decades. Winfrey has said of King, "There is not a better human being in the world as far as I'm concerned." King serves as editor-at-large for *O, the Oprah Magazine*.

8. **Tia Mowry and Tamera Mowry**
   As identical twins, the Mowry sisters were destined to be close from day one. They acted together as teens on the 1990s sitcom *Sister, Sister*, graduated from the same college with matching degrees, and starred for three seasons on a reality show about their lives as adults.

9. **Tyra Banks and Kimora Lee Simmons**
   Banks and Simmons were just teenagers when they met, both modeling for Chanel. They've remained friends for more than twenty-five years, and Banks is godmother to Simmons's oldest daughter.

10. **Queen Latifah and Jada Pinkett Smith**
    The Queen and Pinkett Smith starred in the 1996 movie *Set It Off* and still count each other among their closest friends. Pinkett Smith served as an executive producer on her friend's eponymous talk show and has said, "When I think about Latifah, I think about a woman who makes me feel loved."

Don't Cash Crop
on My Cornrows

BY AMANDLA STENBERG

THE FOLLOWING TRANSCRIPT COMES FROM A PREVIOUSLY PUBLISHED VIDEO
BY AMANDLA STENBERG, WHICH CAN BE VIEWED AT AMANDLA.TUMBLR.COM.

So black hair has always been an essential component of black culture. Black hair requires upkeep in order for it to grow and remain healthy, so black women have always done their hair. It's just a part of our identity: braids, locs, twists and cornrows, et cetera.

Cornrows are a really functional way of keeping black textured hair unknotted and neat, but like with style. So you can see why hair is such a big part of hip-hop and rap culture. These are styles of music which African American communities created in order to affirm our identities and our voices.

In the early 2000s, you saw many R&B stars wearing cornrows: Alicia Keys, Beyoncé, R. Kelly, and many more.

As hip-hop became more and more popular integrated into pop culture, so did black culture. Eminem's album went four times platinum, and he achieved immense success in hip-hop world. Black culture had become popular.

As the early 2000s turned into the 2010s, white people began to wear clothing and accessories associated with hip-hop. More and more celebrities could be seen wearing cornrows and braids and even grills. So by 2013, the fashion world had adopted cornrows as well. Cornrows and braids were seen on high-fashion runways, for brands like Marchesa and Alexander McQueen, and magazines had editorial campaigns featuring cornrows as a new urban hairstyle.

Riff Raff came onto the scene, a suburban white middle-class man who almost ironically took on a blackcent and wore braids and gold teeth. And then James Franco took inspiration from Riff Raff for the creation of the character Alien in *Spring Breakers*. Hip-hop stars and icons adopted black culture as a way of being edgy and gaining attention.

In 2013, Miley Cyrus twerks and uses black women as props, and in 2014, in one of her videos, called "This Is How We Do," Katy Perry uses Ebonics and hand gestures, eats watermelons while wearing cornrows before cutting to a picture of Aretha Franklin.

So as you can see, cultural appropriation was rampant.

Not only were white people becoming rappers, but they were also excelling in the world of hip-hop. Macklemore and Ryan Lewis's song "Thrift Shop" garnered the number one spot on Billboard's year end for 2013, and then Iggy Azalea's song "Fancy" reached number one the following year. And in May 2014, Forbes released an article titled "Hip-Hop's Unlikely New Star, a White Blonde Australian Woman."

But at the same time, police brutality against blacks came to the forefront. In an incredible movement ignited by the murders of Trayvon Martin, Michael Brown, Tamir Rice, Eric Garner, and many others, people began to protest institutionalized racism by marching and using social media. Celebrities spread awareness and shared condolences. Or at least some did, as Azealia Banks, a black female rapper pointed out.

As Azealia Banks observed in her tweets, white musicians who participated in hip-hop culture and adopted "blackness," Iggy Azalea in particular, failed to speak on the racism that comes along with black identity.

Banks and Azalea feuded on Twitter until Banks participated in an interview on New York's Hot 97: "I have a problem when you're trying to like say that it's hip-hop and you're trying to like put it like up against black culture like it's like cultural smudging, is what I see. All it says to white kids is like, oh yeah, you're great, you're amazing, you can do whatever you put your mind to. And it says to black kids, you don't have, you don't, not even shit you've created for yourself. And it makes me upset."

That itself is what is so complicated when it comes to black culture. I mean the line between cultural appropriation and cultural exchanges is always going to be blurred, but here is the thing. Appropriation occurs when a style leads to racist generalizations or stereotypes where it originated but is deemed as high fashion, cool, or funny when the privileged take it for themselves. Appropriation occurs when the appropriator is not aware of the deep significance of the culture they are partaking in.

Hip-hop stems from a black struggle; it stems from jazz and blues, styles of music which African Americans created to retain [their] humanity in the face of adversity, [music that] stems from songs used during [the period of] slavery and [from the need] to communicate and survive. On a smaller scale but in a similar vein, braids and cornrows are not merely stylistic. They're necessary in order to keep black hair neat.

So I've been seeing this question a lot on social media, and I think it's really relevant: what would America be like if we loved black people as much as we love black culture?

A Conversation about Girls' Stories and Girls' Voices with Laurie Halse Anderson and Courtney Summers

BY KELLY JENSEN

Author Laurie Halse Anderson's groundbreaking and award-winning novel *Speak* opened the doors to talking about sexual violence for an entire generation—and more—of readers, teens, and adults alike. Numerous YA and non-YA titles have broached aspects of sexual assault and rape in the years following, thanks to this book's power in getting the conversation rolling. These books are important because they tackle a topic that we don't talk openly enough about, and they're often a means for girls to find comfort, to find hope, and to find a language to use in describing their experiences.

As the conversation around sexual violence has grown and the YA canon of resilience literature has expanded, we've seen how deeply affecting and widely ranging those experiences can be. We've seen authors engaging in tough conversations in ways that lend voice to those who are often voiceless. Likewise, we've seen the conversation move from one of silence to one of exposure.

Rape culture is at the heart of Courtney Summers's *All the Rage*. It's difficult not to see how it parallels Anderson's YA classic. Where *Speak* explores silence around sexual assault, *All the Rage* takes a razor-sharp lens to what it means to be a victim in a world that will go out of its way to discredit your story when you speak up about it.

Inspired by a growing body of work exploring the depths of sexual violence, I wanted to put Laurie and Courtney on the hot seat. What's changed in the last decades when it comes to how we're talking about sexual violence? What's remained the same? And more, why is it important to talk about girls' voices and their stories? This conversation is powerful.

Speak came out in 1999, and All the Rage was released in 2015. Both books explore sexual assault. Speak broke ground in how it looked at the silence surrounding the crime; All the Rage explores the ramifications of rape culture and victim shaming. Let's talk about how the conversation surrounding sexual assault has or hasn't changed in the last decade and a half. Has it? If so, how? Are we getting better, worse, or staying about the same?

COURTNEY SUMMERS: I was thirteen when *Speak* came out and around that age when I read it. That was my introduction to your work, Laurie, and it was the first book I can remember that really helped me grasp what consent is and what it isn't. I'm certain I'd seen movies and TV shows that broached or skimmed the subject of rape, but the intensity of Melinda's point of view was eye-opening for me as a teen. *Speak* is as relevant now as it was when it was first published; rape culture marches on, and victim-shaming continues to happen. It's an ongoing problem, which is why authors are still writing about it today. It's why I'm writing about it today. I do think the conversation surrounding sexual violence has changed, especially in terms of how and where we're having it. The Internet and the advent of social media have expanded the space where we talk about these things for better and for worse. We're able to raise awareness and rally around victims and survivors in large numbers, in real time. We have a direct line of communication where we can challenge and call out the way media and entertainment cover and portray stories about sexual violence. But these same avenues are also available to and used by voices who perpetuate rape culture and blame victims.

LAURIE HALSE ANDERSON: It's helpful to expand the time frame. My story and the story of *Speak* intersect the path of American feminism in some fascinating places.

I was raped in 1975, when I was thirteen years old. I lived in a world shaped by adults who had gone through the Depression and WWII. Those adults had been raised by people with late-Victorian attitudes. (My grandmother liked to talk about what it felt like to her as a ten-year-old when her mother voted for the first time.) People a half generation older than me were protesting the Vietnam War, advocating for civil rights, and birthing the second wave of feminism that brought conversations about sexuality and reproductive rights into the national spotlight.

I wrote *Speak* in 1996–1997, as a mother whose daughters were entering adolescence. The book and then the movie came out as my kids were going through high school and college. Now I am a grandmother who just finished the graphic novel adaptation of *Speak*.

There has been some progress; the fact that books like ours are published and read, and that we can have conversations like this are shining examples. But it's a two-steps-forward, one-step-back, shuffling progress. Some days it feels that for every two steps forward, we stumble back three. We are nowhere near wage equality for women, especially for women of color. Advances in technology and social media have brought new sophistication and appalling reach for the asshats who seek to shame, harass, or threaten women and girls. And the rate of sexual assault has changed very little.

The patriarchy is still going balls to the walls. Sadly.

Some of the most positive developments I've seen recently are the conversations about privilege in American culture. As we confront and question who controls the narrative, and thus, controls the public version about which lives matter, we will make more significant progress in reducing the number of sexual assaults, and increasing support for victims, and prosecuting and jailing rapists.

I am also hopeful that as the women and men growing up in a world with robust YA literature become parents, we will finally have a generation that is not afraid to talk to their children about all aspects of human sexuality. I suspect that children who grow up in homes where there are ongoing conversations about consent are less likely to become rapists and more likely to approach sexual intimacy in a healthy and informed way.

One of the criticisms leveraged at both of your books—and others that tackle sexual assault—is that these books are, in essence, "rape books." Why do we need "rape books" still? Why are authors still writing about this?

CS: *All the Rage* isn't my first time writing about sexual violence, and I've received comments expressing disappointment about how I'm writing "another rape book." More than once it's been said to me that we already have "enough" literature on this topic—like there's some kind of set number [of books], and we're way past it now. The question of why I would write about sexual violence always surprises me, because fiction so often reflects what is happening in the world around us. That so many authors are writing about this should be a big indication to people that we live in a rape culture. And if we're silent about it, if we turn a blind eye to it, we won't break the cycle. Books about difficult and upsetting subject matter often facilitate discussion and raise awareness. We need to do both if we want to see anything change.

LHA: I reject the label of "rape book" because that's an oversimplification of the story. *Speak* is centered on a rape victim, but it is the story of her struggle to find her power to speak up and be heard. Using labels like "rape book" distances people from the narratives. The use of the label is often a flag that signals the speaker's discomfort talking about sexual assault and/or sexuality in general. Furthermore, labels like "rape book" fall into the same category as "chick lit," "knit lit," and "mommy lit." Patronizing labels applied to books written by women are an attempt to denigrate the work. They piss me all the way off.

But to get to your larger point . . . The role of the artist in society is to hold up a mirror. We'll stop writing about rape when rapists stop sexually assaulting people.

(Maybe I should write a book about the crap that women writers have to put up with, too.)

An interesting parallel between your books is the idea of re-claiming one's self after being a victim. In *Speak*, Melinda finds herself through her art; in *All the Rage*, Romy finds that self in her routine of applying red lipstick and red nail polish. Their art becomes more than armor for them. It becomes identity. Can you talk about this a bit?

CS: In *All the Rage*, Romy has a lot of difficulty processing her trauma, and the routine of putting on her lipstick and nail polish is what helps her to compartmentalize it. It's how she separates herself from what happened to her enough that she can get through her day. The makeup is also how Romy directs the way people look at her. She is inescapably "the Girl Who Cried Rape" within her community, but when people see her, they see the red first. And even though it's just for a moment, it's a moment where she has the tiniest bit of control over their perception of her. The makeup, for Romy, is about controlling her narrative as much as she possibly can when so many others have taken it from her and twisted it.

LHA: I love the way you described the process: "Their art becomes more than armor for them. It becomes identity." Art helps us process emotions and experiences before we can find the words. This is particularly important for trauma survivors. Teenagers—who are so vulnerable because the world is crashing toward them at a million miles an hour—seek armor wherever they can find it. Art (visual, music, literature, dance) is a healthy form of armor because it creates in the soul the opportunity for growth and transformation. When teens don't have access to art (I'm looking at you, budget-cutting school boards and state governments), they turn to unhealthy armor, like drugs and booze; anything to diminish the confusion and pain.

A key difference in your books is that Melinda in *Speak* doesn't speak up about her assault immediately. Romy (*All the Rage*) is open with her peers, as well as with her parents, about being raped. And yet, in both stories, they are girls who are not believed. This isn't about the "telling."

What's at work here? Why are we as a culture so quick to dismiss victims' testimonies and girls' lived experiences?

CS: We live in a world that polices the way girls dress in schools specifically so boys can learn in "distraction-free" environments. We live in a world that actively wants to deny women reproductive rights. We live in a world where a woman's accomplishments matter less than how perfect she looks and a world where it's totally acceptable to tear a woman apart if she doesn't look perfect enough. We live in a world that gets outraged over an all-female *Ghostbusters* reboot—and all that's just scratching the surface. It would be nearly impossible not to internalize this stuff, so when I see victim blaming, when I hear or read comments that victims of sexual violence deserve or ask for it, I see that as an extension and consequence of a world that inundates us daily with the message that girls don't matter or, if they matter at all, they matter less.

LHA: This is such an important point to consider and Courtney has brought up a lot of good material. I'll add this: the testimony of victims is disregarded because if it is taken seriously, then the rapists must be arrested, prosecuted, and jailed. And that means a whole lot of guys who don't like to think of themselves (or their sons) as rapists have to face an ugly truth and deal with the consequences.

America keeps telling itself two lies: 1) that all rapists are bad guys in the bushes with a gun, and 2) that it's not rape if (fill in the blank) the victim was wearing sexy clothes, or was on a date with the rapist, or was dancing provocatively, or was drunk or high . . . The list of sick rationalizations is long and disgusting.

Rape is most frequently (more than two-thirds of the time) committed by someone that the victim knows. Eighty percent of sexual assaults do not involve a weapon. (These statistics and more can be found at https://rainn.org/statistics.)

American Rape Lie 2A) is that all sexual violence victims are female. While our conversation has focused on assaults of women by men, it is important not to overlook the boys and men who are victims of sexual violence, usually at the hands of other men. Our culture blames and won't listen to those victims, either, which has horrible implications for their healing.

CS: It's definitely important that we not overlook male victims and survivors of sexual violence and the appalling lack of resources and help available to them. Laurie's right—it all points to a culture that willfully fails victims because it's easier and more comfortable to look away.

You both wrote stories where the main character struggles, metaphorically and literally, with finding her voice after she's been ostracized and shunned by her peers. Yet both narratives highlight the importance of speaking your truth. What do you hope readers will gain from your characters' struggles and triumphs when it comes to finding their own voices?

CS: It was important for me to highlight how difficult and risky it can be to speak your truth. In *All the Rage*, Romy reaches a point where it's what she must do, and it takes a lot of courage for her to do it—and it remains a risk. But if a girl chooses silence, that's not an act of cowardice. It's often an act of self-preservation in response to not having a safe place. I want readers to walk away from the book understanding why, for many girls, speaking up is not always a viable option and knowing how critical it is to create spaces that are safe enough for others so they can speak up. I want them to take a look at the spaces around them and ask whether they're part of the solution or part of the problem.

LHA: That is a brilliant answer, Courtney!

I only have a couple of things to add to it. Finding the courage to speak your truth is one of the most difficult lessons for teens to learn. Many adults are still struggling with the wounds and scars of their adolescent transition because they have not been able to claim their power and speak that truth.

One of the positive developments of social media is the increased opportunity to speak up, speak out, and listen as others speak. This has brought a hideous backlash in the form of online harassment, death threats, SWATting [where an individual's name and location are used to make prank calls to emergency lines], etc. I continue to marvel at how pathetic the lives of online trolls must be if they find pleasure in puking online-hatred. Part of me wants to punch them in the throat. Another part tries to understand who they were at age three, at ten, at thirteen. How did they become so warped? Who hurt them? How do we ensure the safety of all people who deserve the ability to speak their truth without fear? How do we help move the culture forward?

Why do you write girls' stories? Why do they matter?

CS: Writing about girls is something I've had to defend over the course of my career. I've been told by prospective readers that they're interested in my work, but the only thing holding them back from picking it up is my choice of main character; they think they're just not going to be able to relate to a female protagonist because she is female. Whatever I choose to write about, whether it be sexual violence, girl-bullying, or depression—I will invariably run across comments that reduce the very real struggles girls go through in every possible way. Girls are drama queens, girls have petty catfights, girls in crisis are attention-seeking, and on and on. This is what I'm writing against when I write girl stories. But I've been fortunate to hear from girl readers who have seen themselves in my books, who have felt less alone because of that, and many who have been inspired to write their own stories—and that's what I'm writing for. Girls' stories matter because girls matter.

LHA: Because I matter. My daughters matter. My mother and grandmothers mattered. You, Courtney, and you, Kelly, matter. Every girl, every woman deserves agency, recogni-

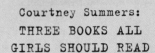

Courtney Summers: THREE BOOKS ALL GIRLS SHOULD READ

1. *We Should All Be Feminists* by Chimamanda Ngozi Adichie
Adapted from her TED talk—every girl should read it. It's a fantastic introduction to feminism and provides a great launching point to discussion about feminism.

2. *Bad Feminist* by Roxane Gay
Roxane Gay is awesome. From the introduction: "These essays are political and they are personal. They are, like feminism, flawed, but they come from a genuine place. [. . .] I'm raising my voice to show all the ways we have room to want more, to do better." Her essays give girls a lot to think about, especially moving forward.

3. *Odd Girl Out: The Hidden Culture of Aggression in Girls* by Rachel Simmons
This book helped me understand how and why my friends and I expressed our anger toward one another the ways we did in school. Girls are constantly encouraged to be nice at the expense of themselves, and Rachel Simmons explores the consequences of that here.

Laurie Halse Anderson: THREE BOOKS ALL GIRLS SHOULD READ

1. *Bad Feminist* by Roxane Gay **gets my vote, too.**

2. Anything by Tamora Pierce, because she is a great writer of strong female characters and because genre fiction can help us see our world with new eyes.

3. *The Handmaid's Tale* by Margaret Atwood, because that could really happen here, and we must all fight to prevent it.

tion, and respect just as every boy and man does. Respecting all lives as equal and important is the next great leap for our culture to take.

How can we be there and support girls? How can we advance the conversations about sexism and what that entails? Where can we make change?

CS: I firmly believe if you support girls, you should loudly declare yourself a supporter of girls. Don't take it for granted that they know; let them know you're there for them. We should always be aware there is room for improvement in the way we approach conversations about sexism. To improve, we need to be able look closely at ourselves and at any biases we've internalized, and how those biases might negatively impact what we're doing or run counter to what we're trying to achieve. That's not always an easy thing to do, but it's necessary. Let's think about the way we're gendering books. Let's stop. Think about the way we mock and dismiss the reading tastes of teenage girls. Let's not. If you organize public events, look at whom you're inviting to speak at them. Are women represented? If you're a writer, be conscious of the way you represent women in your work. We should take opportunities to celebrate female authors and female characters. These things add up, and they make a difference.

LHA: The best way to support girls is to listen to them. Give them the space and security they need to tell their stories, to ask their questions. We also must surround them with many and varied examples of women choosing to live the lives they want, instead of shutting off their brains and living out the hollow script that some segments of society want them to follow.

THIS PIECE WAS PREVIOUSLY PUBLISHED ON BOOKRIOT.COM.

RELATIONSHIPS

RELATIONSHIPS matter.

Whether you believe in having a lot of friends or just a few close ones,

whether you choose to date or not to date, whether you're close to your parents or you're quite independent, all of those choices and decisions can be guided by feminism in some capacity.

As seen throughout this discussion, having the ability to make your own choices and acting on that ability are what feminism is all about.

Our feminist beliefs and actions are only strengthened through the relationships that flourish, as well as the ones we let wither away. Whether it's through the way we learn about ourselves and our heritage, how we defend and support the people in our lives who matter, or even the words we choose when we talk about other individuals, the ways we connect with one another matter.

Girl Lessons

BY SARAH McCARRY

In third grade, you play queen and her warriors: you the queen, boys your loyal army, David H. your brave liege. When it rains, you imagine the water in the field behind the elementary school is the blood of the slain. Your will is strongest, and your knights obey your every command: slay dragons, fourth-graders, and Jenny O. who told you she invited you to her eighth birthday party only because her parents made her ask everyone in the class. Already you are learning a long memory for hurt.

In fifth grade, your legions forsake you. Their defection is wordless, unanimous, instantaneous. "Is David your boyfriend now?" sneers Jenny O., and you understand you have done something wrong, that it is your own body that has driven away these loyal companions, the only friends you had. The only friends you will have for a long time. Now you have no friends at all. Jenny O. shows the straps of her new bra to her lieutenants, doe-eyed and sleek-haired doctors' daughters, in the girls' bathroom between classes. "*Lez,*" she hisses to you when she catches you looking. You don't know what the word means, but you can tell by the way she spits it that it's something you shouldn't be. That year David H. will bring you a bracelet in a box and leave it on your desk with a note that says, *I love you.* You will understand immediately that it is wrong to be loved in this way by David H., who is so poor he gets free school lunches, whose soft belly spills over the elastic waistband of his cheap trousers. David H., who shows up twice monthly at school with black eyes (from walking into doors, falling down staircases—you were never allowed to go over to his house when you were friends). David H., who taught you to play Dungeons & Dragons before your mother caught you out and told you the game was satanic. David H., who read the *Dragonlance Chronicles* in order with you, who also longed to be the sinister, tormented, all-powerful mage Raistlin (it would never have occurred to you to want to be one of the girl characters, who cried and had sex; who knew which of these was worse).

Jenny O. is loved by Kevin S., whose parents are also doctors and who is a rising star of the baseball team, whose thick dark hair falls in his face when he laughs. Kevin S.'s eyes are a light clear blue, and his lanky body already moves with the easy grace of the blessed. Kevin S. pins you up against the wall of the school once when no one is looking and, hot breath against your face, snarls, "What are you looking at?" You never tell; what would you say? You know better than to look. After David H. brings you the bracelet, you will never speak to him again, though you'll keep it for twenty years. Every time you look at the cheap glass gemstones and tarnished metal chain, a hot knife of shame will run through your heart until finally you'll bring yourself to throw it away.

This is how you first learn what it is to be a girl. Soon, there'll be more incidents. Teachers in the halls, asking if you're sure you want to wear that to school, if you shouldn't go home and change. "Aren't you cold in that, Sarah?" Mr. K. says, his mouth an ugly twist (you're wearing engineer's overalls, two sizes too big, and a tank top that bares your shoulders; you have no idea what you've done wrong). Joe R. in physics, who sits at the lab table behind you and asks you every day in a low, mocking hiss if you're wearing a bra (you'll fail the final with his eyes on the back of your neck; girls are stupid). Keith P., who will tell you some guy might actually like you if you didn't make people feel stupid ("It's not my fault you're dumb," you'll think to say days later, long after it's too late). Chris R., golden child of your freshman class, sailing down the halls of your school, surrounded by a cloud of laughing, beautiful girls, who'll throw the dodgeball at your head on purpose in PE and write *Too bad you're skinny and ugly* in your yearbook (words that will stay with you for decades, long after you have forgotten Chris R.'s real name and face and why you even cared whether he thought you were pretty in the first place).

This is how you decide that to be a girl in a girl's body is a target. There are so many ways to get it wrong. There are so many ways to be unwanted, to be wanted too much. This is how you learn how to have contempt for the body that is yours, how to live outside it, how to erase your own desires and your wants, bury over your raw and fragile heart.

This is how you learn to choose boys.

The boys who have done you harm are surrounded by girls you will choose never to be. Girls who are disgusting, who bleed and weep and wail. Girls who spend too much time in the bathroom. Girls who are never ready on time. Girls who titter, who are soft, who wear pretty clothes that are easily dirtied, girls in hoop earrings and perfect wings of black eyeliner, girls who don't know what's cool. Girls who read the wrong books, twirl their hair around, are pursued, are hunted. You will remake yourself into something else: a boys' girl, a tough girl, a girl without needs or feelings, a girl who wisecracks and drinks whiskey in the backseat of cars, a girl cool as the first frost in winter, a girl so *totally* unlike other girls. If you cannot be loved and safe, you will be clever, mean, a girl as vicious as the serrated edge of a hunting knife. If you cannot be pretty, you will disdain beauty and its trappings. If you cannot be heard, you will be silent on purpose. You will find your knights again, a different set of boys, this time united against a common enemy: the softness and the fragility of girls, of anything girlish within you, of anything girlish in any other girl. Against girls who are sad and silly and weeping (you don't cry), girls who complain (you protest nothing), girls who make demands (you never ask). This time, however, you will not be queen. Some of these boys will never even know your name.

Toughness is synonymous with boys, but more important, so is freedom, and freedom is what you want. Look at the freedoms of boys: to move around in their bodies without the commentary of others. To take up space. To boast, be clever, ask questions. To assume they are correct. To walk alone in the dark. To speak and know that they will be heard. To have faith that room will be made. To be taken seriously. Your physics teacher will tell Joe R., who sits behind you and asks about your bra, that he can have a promising career if he applies himself ("I think that's a little over your head," he'll say to you when he sees James Gleick's *Chaos* on your desk). To be a boy is a preferable condition. You are not a boy, but hating girls is almost the same thing. Isn't it? That's what boys do. You can do it, too.

You make yourself superior. Superior in your silence, your lack of want. You take up no space. You quit eating and do not name aloud the hunger that rages every day in your belly. You are not like other girls. You are not like other girls ("You are not like other girls," the boys you run with will tell you, and you will try not to let them see you preen under the glancing light of their approval). You learn their books and their language. You laugh at their jokes. You listen to their stories, sit blank-eyed on their couches while they play video games, pass them your English notes. You keep their secrets. You use the words they use about other girls in order to assure yourself that they will never use those words about you. You make yourself into nothingness, a ghost conjured into being only through the desires of boys, the rules of boys, the ideas of boys. *You're not like other girls.* If you turn sideways, you are so thin, you can almost disappear. If you are good enough at this, you will be safe.

You are never quite good enough at it, as it turns out. You were never, in their company, safe.

It will take you long, lonely years, but one day you will grow tired. Tired of boys, tired of contempt, and then where will you be? All these girls around you with their stories and their lives, the solace of one another, and you will be as far away from them as an anthropologist among a foreign people, curious but unable to make contact. Have faith: you will learn. In college, you'll live with a girl who climbs mountains by herself, who isn't pretty and doesn't care, who isn't pretty and is also loved. You, who's starved yourself into nothing, who's been silent so long, you can hardly remember language, will blossom like a flower in the light of her care. She eats when she is hungry, picks fights when she is correct, says no. She knows other women: women who care about clothes and women who don't; women who read the same books you do and women who read books that are better than the ones boys gave you; women who paint and cook and write and go out walking in the woods under the pale stars. The girl you'll live with cries when she is sad and laughs when she is happy and is brave most of the time but not always and burns fiercely with the light of her own dreams. "I don't care about that," she'll say at a party one night, when some boy starts to tell a story about himself. He'll wander off in a huff, and she'll turn to you.

"I'd rather listen to you," she'll say to you. "How come you never talk?" Your heart stammering in your chest, your blood singing in your veins like a living thing. Your own tongue, thick with disuse, unused to language other than the lie you thought was the only option.

Here's your own voice, sleeping. Here's your life as a girl, a thing you've never before let live. Here's your own road, unrolling before you like a promise.

Well, you'll think, and she'll take your hand, catching the spark flaring to life in your eyes. *Before you, no one asked.*

And you will open your girl's mouth to speak.

"A girl who does not grow up to become a princess is doomed to become a witch" - Revolutionary Girl Utena

When I was a little kid, "Beauty and the Beast" was my favorite story.

The story of a girl (who also loved to read), who was the only one who could see the good in a monster boy.

When I was fifteen, I fell head over heels in love with a boy on the other side of the country, and we connected through forums: roleplaying characters, telling stories.

Slowly, over the course of weeks and months, an entire universe came into being.

But you SAID you still loved me! How could you just... make out with someone else like that?!?!?!

It was not the first conversation like that. Nor would it be the last.

We weren't dating. We were in love. We met at the "wrong time." We were "best friends."

Whatever WE were, it was never the same again. That universe we made together, those stories, were over. Forever.

Well, thank god we don't stay in high school forever. I graduated, moved to New York, and got really into doing Tarot and other witchy things for fun.

For the first time, I had a lot of friends who were Asian women, and realized that we shared many of the same experiences.

Including the fact that, somewhere along the line, many of us had had partners who were obsessed with our "Asian-ness".

In Tarot, The Hanged Man can represent an emotional release and learning to accept what is.

The short comics I had made so far, about being an "Asian-American woman, were enormously cathartic and healing, as I found power in the fact that I was not alone in what I went through.

But with the release came the rage and the realization that maybe I meant nothing to K. That maybe I was just a fetish.

The stories we'd told and the worlds we made had been so important to me, and the thought that it was tainted by the fact that he only did those things with me because I was a cute Asian girl made me despair.

The only great creative partnership I'd ever had, and it was with a guy who saw me as a knockoff Amy Tan?!

It took me quite awhile to get off the tree.

My friends and I had gone to this event solely to be snarky, petty and mean.

Afterwards, I became convinced that the universe has a sense of humor. Like, of course I would run into K...

yes, I did wear a cape that day→

...at an AMY TAN reading.

He seemed genuinely happy to see me. I made sure I expressed a cool air of indifference that hid my white-hot rage.

And then, afterwards, it all came pouring out. He was taken aback. He had such good memories!

To his credit, he heard me out, and he gave me a sincere apology at having been a bad friend, all those years ago.

But it made me realize that he remembered the relationship so differently. HE never doubted his love. Me... how do you separate the real affection from the creepy fetish? Can you really? Should you try?

I don't have an answer to anything, really. All I know was that, for me, this was the moment to get off the tree. What's the point in trying to convince him he had a gross fetish, when he couldn't even remember half of the crap he said, all those years ago? He wasn't some prince trapped in the body of a beast, changeable with the wave of a witch's wand.

My first true love was a white guy who will never fully grasp the implications of what he said to me when we were both teenagers! He had let those words drain from his memory long ago, while it's stayed with me, repeated to me, in many ways.

Me love you long time.

So, I was JUST in Japan...

This wasn't some scripted YA novel.

What was there left to do, but to say "Okay, whatever," and walk away from trying to separate what was real and what was a fetish, and move on?

So I didn't get my grandiose closure. Big deal. Instead, I got a new creative partnership with one of my best friends, Suzanne. Together, we schemed and brainstormed.

We stayed up late, texting ideas. She wrote all the scripts, and I did the art.

Our new webcomic was received with incredible support and excitement, by people who had only read the first few pages!

A bright new universe, where ghosts came over for Thanksgiving dinner, where and witches and werewolves grew up as childhood friends, had come into being.

And this time, it was here to stay.

Corny Won't Kill Your Cred: Rearview Mirror Reflections on Feminism and Romance

BY SIOBHAN VIVIAN

Hi, Siobhan,

It's me. Or, rather, it's you. I'm you, Siobhan, and I'm writing you this letter from twenty-four years in the future. If I've done my math correctly, as I write this, you're about to enter your freshman year of high school.

Don't worry! Everything's fine. Nobody's dead! And I'm not going to ask you to save the world or anything like that.

I want to talk to you about a decision you're about to make. Or, to look at it another way, I want to explain (with the benefit of time and wisdom) a decision I made for us. The purpose of this letter isn't to *Back to the Future* you into somehow altering the entire trajectory of your existence. Your future looks really, realllllllly good.

It's more like I want to amplify the tiny feminist voice that's already there, deep down inside you. It gets way louder as you get older, but this letter is a nice shortcut to understanding your strength and power and future badassness. So think of me as something between an older sister and a fairy godmother with a feminist magic wand.

Are you feeling a little weird about this? Sorry. I know just the thing to put your mind at ease. Because I know you love compliments, here are a few qualities that are wonderful about you.

First, bravo on the decision that boys are not as important to you as your friends. This is a terrific feminist mind-set, and a rare one to possess in high school. Boys come and go rapidly, and the girl friendships you care about now are the friendships you'll still care about when you are much, much older.

Second, Spoiler Alert: you will be voted Most Unique in your senior yearbook. Isn't that cool? It's because you don't think twice about cutting off all your hair and bleaching it platinum blond. Or buying a leopard-print prom dress when everyone else is going for pastels. You don't automatically love something just because other people say to. You find your own music, you create your own scene, and you define your own fashion sense. You have a bravery in you that your peers admire. Hence the superlative win!

Last, your sense of humor is one of your most sparkly qualities, Siobhan. You can make almost everyone laugh. Your humor is your passport to all different social groups. A funny girl is always a welcome addition, and you often use your humor to put other people at ease.

But here's the thing: those three amazing qualities, the seeds to your future feminist ideology, can also have a dark side to them, especially when it comes to romance. And that's kind of what I want to talk to you about, girl to girl.

At this moment in your life, you've French-kissed three boys and you've touched one penis (though you didn't see that penis very clearly, because you removed your glasses before hanging out with R.G.—you thought glasses made you look ugly).

Brace yourself, Siobhan. In a few months, you're going to lose your virginity.

I know. It's a big jump. Huge even.

You will date a boy who is a sophomore. There is no courtship to your relationship, no wooing. His friends date your friends, and the convenience and that social proximity win out over your feeling kind of *meh* about him.

And just a few short weeks later, you'll have a choice to make. His mom will be out running errands when you visit him after school, and he will wonder if you want to have sex with him. That's exactly how he'll ask.

"Hey. Do you maybe want to have sex?"

The choice you make greatly influences how you view romance, love, and your feelings about genuine emotion for the rest of your adolescence. I'm going to tell you how it played out. Maybe, after reading this letter, you'll make a different decision than I did.

Or maybe you won't. Which is fine, too.

Okay. So. I said yes to L.S. Actually, my answer was something more like, "Yeah, sure, whatever."

I knew I wasn't in love with him. Not even close. But I thought to myself, *Why not?* in the same practical, unemotional way that I got together with L.S. in the first place.

The sex wasn't terrible, but it definitely wasn't amazing. Mostly, it felt surreal. Like . . . *now I am a person who has had sex.* Before I wasn't, and now I was. I actually laughed out loud at my new "secret" when Dad picked me up later that day. The quotes are intentional, because I immediately regarded losing my virginity, which was done safely and consensually, as no big deal. I jumped straight into the funniness of it.

The relationship with L.S. didn't last another month. In fact, we were already kind of on the way out. When we did break up, I wasn't sure how to feel about him, or what we had done. I really struggled, wondering if losing my virginity could still be a special moment if it wasn't with someone special and I hadn't particularly cared one way or the other.

In that confusion, my views on romance got rewired. I interpreted my lack of emotion as a very feminist, even adult, mind-set—especially when I compared myself to the girls I saw in the hallways, making up and breaking up every other day. I didn't expect much from L.S. because I knew the emotional limits of a high school relationship.

And from that moment on, I started to feel comfortable only with non-traditional romantic gestures. I liked moments that felt more like inside jokes, "romance with a wink" moments, poking fun of the artifice of high school romance. I didn't want to take any of it seriously. I didn't want to be emotional about it. I wanted to be strong. A feminist.

Obviously, I enjoyed the nice things boys did for me. But the more irreverent they were, the more I embraced them. So instead of flowers, I paraded around a carton of cigarettes a boy bought for me on my fifteenth birthday. Or I sighed with swoony, girlish delight when a boy paid for me to get my cartilage pierced in the West Village. There was one boyfriend who, on Valentine's Day, bought me the corniest card he could find at the drugstore and completely defaced it, rubbing away the pink paper inside with an eraser so it left behind a hand flipping the bird. I thought this was so ridiculous, so hilarious, so untraditional, so perfectly me.

I liked redefining what teen romance could be. And I did it in a very showy way to let my peers know that I was making up my own rules. This, the control I was exerting over my heart, also felt very feminist to me.

But as funny as I was, deep down I didn't feel very confident. And this is still, even for me (us?) in the future, a thing I (we?) struggle with. It's the weird dichotomy of being an insecure extrovert. I am still more comfortable putting on a show than revealing my true self to people. Though I make jokes about myself, I also feel there's truth to the things I say. But because I say them first, it feels like I control them, own them. It is 10,000 percent a defense of my insecurities.

I know you kind of already know this, but it's really true.

Also, sometimes I am too quick to joke about serious things, because I haven't quite yet figured out how to deal with tough emotional stuff. And the issue with that is when I don't take myself seriously, I don't make other people take me seriously, either.

Here's what I mean. After college, I moved across the country and made friends with a new group of girls. One afternoon, with beach chairs set out on the driveway blacktop, we all shared stories about the time we lost our virginity.

I, of course, went first. Because we have always been a "go first" girl, with very few filters and even fewer triggers of embarrassment. And I told the story of L.S. Actually, I performed it like a comedy routine. I played the memory for laughs. The story behind losing my virginity had become as much of a joke as anything else romantic in high school, and I wanted these new friends to understand exactly how seriously I took it all.

But one girl didn't laugh. She looked like she felt bad for me.

She had the kind of saccharine-sweet experience that definitely would have made high school Siobhan roll her eyes. She lost her virginity on prom night to a boy she had dated for a year. He rented a special hotel room for them, bought flowers, made a playlist of their favorite songs.

And I immediately cracked a joke about how corny that sounded.

The girl blinked a few times. She didn't get what I found so funny. There wasn't anything performative or fake about her emotions. She *had* been in love. And though she and that guy were no longer together, it was still a special moment she could hold on to and feel proud of.

And really, there was nothing corny about that.

Leaving that day, I went over again and again the details of my first time. I allowed myself to stray from the script, away from the way I jokingly told that story. I forced myself to look at it objectively.

My experience had been fine. It wasn't traumatic, and I wasn't forced.

But I wasn't in love. Not even close.

I said yes to L.S. because I was afraid that no one else would think of me in that way. And that was not a position of power. There was nothing strong about that choice. It was a reaction to my very deep-seated weakness.

All this to say, Siobhan, you turn out okay. And you don't have any regrets. You are not scarred by losing your virginity to L.S. And, honestly, I still think it is mostly a good idea not to place serious expectations on any high school relationships beyond having fun in the moment.

But that shouldn't mean that you don't require authenticity, both from within yourself and whomever you're romantically involved with. You don't have to settle for the easy, funny, right-now thing . . . unless that is truly what you want. Being honest with yourself and your partner is the feminist position to take. It's hard—maybe even impossible—for anyone to know that at your age, so don't feel bad. And you shouldn't worry. If you can't do it now, you will eventually get to a place where you can.

Love you,
Me

GREAT GIRL FRIENDSHIPS IN FICTION

1. *Black Girl in Paris*, by Shay Youngblood

   Twenty-six-year-old aspiring writer Eden follows in the footsteps of her heroes James Baldwin, Richard Wright, and Langston Hughes, landing in Paris with nothing but two hundred dollars and a handful of really big dreams to her name. Along the way, she meets up with a wily and complicated girl grifter who teaches her to survive by her wits on the streets of the City of Light.

2. *The Elementals*, by Francesca Lia Block

   Spooky and surreal, *The Elementals* is the story of Ariel Silverman, who's consumed by the quest to find out what happened to her best friend, Jeni, who vanished without trace years earlier. Ariel and Jeni's friendship defines the course of Ariel's life and leads her to the house of three mysterious strangers who may or may not be helping her find the truth.

3. *Girl Walking Backwards*, by Bett Williams

   All Skye wants to do is survive high school, which is tough when your mom is nuts, your suicidal goth girlfriend is cheating on you, and your life is falling apart. But then Skye meets Mol, a tough and sweet-hearted girl who teaches her what real friendship looks like.

4. *The Saskiad*, by Brian Hall

   Twelve-year-old Saskia White lives with her hippie mother on a run-down former commune in upstate New York. Saskia's brilliant, solitary, and obsessed with Homer's Odyssey and her best friend, Jane Singh. But when her long-lost charismatic environmental-activist father swoops unexpectedly back into her life, he comes between Saskia and Jane in a way she never could have imagined.

5. *Uses for Boys*, by Erica Lorraine Scheidt

   Anna and her mother are everything to each other until her mother starts chasing one man after the next, leaving Anna to fend for herself. Like her mom, Anna seeks solace in boys, but it's when she makes friends with a troubled runaway named Toy that she starts to take her own story seriously.

Faith and the Feminist

BY KAYE MIRZA

When I was very young, my mother held me on her lap and taught me about feminists—and why they were everything I didn't need to be.

And she was right.

You may not have expected to hear this from me. Many women are horrified, or astonished. They remain blissfully unaware of the connotations behind a movement that should be, must be, settled on a foundation of universal equality and respect. It is an innocence often borne by privilege, and hapless ignorance.

It is an innocence I, and so many other women with marginalized voices and backgrounds and experiences, are not allowed to keep.

As a feminist of faith, I've grown used to being told to take a step back. I've held up banners, given feminism a new battle cry to utilize on social media and in daily conversation through the creation of #YesAllWomen. In spite of that, even former supporters and fellow activists have recoiled when they realize I am a Muslim woman, a woman who proudly wears the hijab and constantly references religious activities.

In spite of that, as soon as I harness my own experience, any contributions from my voice are rendered void.

I've been advised to worry about feminism less and my own individual freedoms more. I've been informed that, as a woman tethered to the outdated concept of religion, I am still firmly under a patriarchal thumb, albeit a divine one. To be taken seriously—to be a real sister, acknowledged by the cause—I should bow my head, unpin my scarf, and allow myself to be the rescue project rather than the active leader.

As long as I practice my faith, to many, I am nothing but a secondhand feminist. It is a bias as deeply steeped and shamefully dark as the machinations of the patriarchy. This prejudice goes hand in hand with the accusation that discussions of any marginalized feminist's own struggles caused by other women are nothing more than derailing.

At my mother's knee, I learned about the demoralization of intersectionality that tainted every narrative of triumph against adversity: how crucial struggles for civil rights were dismissed as derailing, how the rose-tinted stories of the era of suffrage erased marginalized women or set them as far back in the frontlines as they could be pressured to go.

As textbooks focused their coverage on linked arms, marches in Washington, airbrushed smiles on carefully selected stock models, and Rosie the Riveter re-enactors—unified femininity, so long as you kept the right place in line—my eyes were drawn to other pictures just as delicately, painstakingly chosen: veiled women, chained women, silenced women. Women all in black, eyes cast down as though in shame. Their own words were omitted in favor of large captions and words that I quickly learned by the tug of nausea in my stomach to despise: oppressed, brainwashed, chattel, our sisters in need of liberation.

The millennial generation grew up in the shadows of the Twin Towers. We mourned our dead, and we learned who were considered American enough to stand tall and proudly raise their voices for the national anthem . . . and who were to have their patriotism sneered at, their heritage denied and rejected, and their bloodlines brought into question.

The narrative of who I was and what my faith was based upon, what I believed in and preached, and ultimately where I stood as a woman, was not in my hands.

I was continuously cajoled, coaxed, and entreated during my formative years to remove my scarf. What should have been a simple choice from the heart—a layer of modesty, a cloth of comfort as I'd always known it to be—was maligned and used against me.

When I was ten, a woman screamed at me from a car, wheels screeching erratically over a mall parking lot: "Take it off! You should take it off!" It was for my own good, to her. I was a little Muslim girl, holding hands with my perplexed, brown father. I had no voice of my own and no agency beyond what he allowed me with his tender grip and firm steering away from my supposed rescuer's open window.

"Agency" is one of my favorite words. Perhaps because, for so long, it was denied to me—not by my parents, who faithfully pruned weeds threatening to choke my voice, or by my community, who gave me reason to raise said voice with pride and dignity. When I claim my agency, I am claiming my right and authority over my mind, my body, what I choose to wear, how I choose to act and speak and feel and declaim as much and as frequently as I want.

I choose how to present myself. I choose what to believe in.

I choose to be me.

At summer camp when I was thirteen, a fellow camper at the local riding stables admitted that she took my scarf as a reason to fear me, to shun me, to pity me, to see me not as another girl coming into my gawky limbs and forgetting to put on enough sunscreen—but as an Other.

Of course, she was confused. After all, normal, intelligent, informed girls didn't mount horses with cloths wrapped about their necks and over their hair. They were not obliged to break, abruptly and with much whispering, when dusk fell and they were finally allowed to eat after a day of no food or water.

The confession was shy and laced with contrition: she was wrong, and we clasped hands and set it behind us.

I should have set it behind me. Instead, like so many other elbow-awkward, painful experiences, it was tied up in a knot and shoved in the closet of my childhood. So were my beloved riding instructor's questions about how soon I could expect to be dragged, kicking and screaming, into an arranged marriage and whether I feared a *Not without My Daughter* scenario if I went to visit my grandmother overseas.

I could not forget. I did not forget.

As the world was fueled by apprehension and blatant misinformation and propaganda, every experience taught me more about what it meant to be a feminist—and I was sure, in my bones, that I would never claim to be one.

Of course, that was my fault, too. I was too subservient. That is a way that, so very often, my faith has been used against me. It is degrading, debasing, to use the word "submit" in regard to myself and my actions (or so I've been told). It lowers my agency. The idea, the very notion, that a modern woman should choose to prostrate herself five times a day before a divine presence is, to many, one of the reasons that we need to denounce the patriarchy.

Feminism seemed to decry women like me. And so, for all appearances and purposes, I decried feminism. I turned my back on that mystical unicorn that feminism claimed to be, and how it battered at the doors of my identity and my resolve to stay firm to my roots.

This is not where the story ends.

And that is for the simple fact that my faith led me back to feminism.

With every inquiry I could not answer, every triumphant smile over a battle against my resolve seemingly won, I turned to my studies with a fierce determination.

While I was in high school, my textbook used a handful of paragraphs to denounce my religion, deeming it spread by the sword, by the hand of a man who believed women to be less than, other, who left behind a legacy of pain and ignorance.

I did not listen to just that supposed narrative. I sat at the feet of my mother and my teachers, and I wove together the hidden narrative of pride and honor and education, the narrative of a prophet who came to a land where girl children were buried alive, who wept over the indecencies heaped on the heads of mothers and wives, and who invited them to raise their voices alongside men.

I learned the true heritage of the Muslim woman: she who holds tightly to the first revealed verses of her Holy Book—"Read, in the name of God"— she who founded the world's first-known university (Fatima al-Fihri); she who taught male elders and corrected their religious errors (Aishah bint Abu Bakr); she who opens safe spaces (Malala Yousafzai) and campaigns against domestic violence; she who has ascended to the highest political ranks in countries often considered the least educated.

I was fortunate to discover the complex online conversations held within the writing and faith-led communities. Intersectional feminism led me to straddle both without feeling I was compromising or associating with people who did not understand or respect the traits that made me. I belonged, and I continue to belong.

Muslim women made me welcome. They made me belong. I watched in awe as their intellect and eloquence created and maintained a community of continuous growth, development, and hope:

Jennifer Zobair, presenting an anthology solely devoted to feminists of faith and their often-dismissed voices.

Margari Aziza and Namira Ali, marching at Ferguson and creating MuslimARC to challenge issues of racism, prejudice, and erasure within and outside the community.

Zareen Jaffery and Salaam Reads, Laila Alawa, Ayesha Mattu and Nura Maznavi, just a few of the growing surge of voices writing themselves into a one-sided, detractive narrative through online journalism, real stories, heartfelt and humorous experiences—love and light and faith and romance and everything in between, everything that we are so often told is "derailing the important conversations."

These women showed me that I was meant to be here. They showed me that I could be heard, that my voice was not merely one small, tremulous mistake in a continuous current of what is always right and true (even if you know it is not). We are enough. We are strong. We are more than arranged marriages and a supposed lack of education and the assumed patriarchal thumb of organized religion.

A few months after the furor around #YesAllWomen died down, I tentatively rearranged my personal corner of the Internet. I placed that label in my biography: "feminist." And I waited. There were the detractors. There were the belittlers. There were the hateful, closed hearts and finger-wagging shamers that told me, insisted, I should have known better.

But there were the confident reassurances, too.

"Yes, this is our heritage."

"Yes, this is our faith."

"Yes, this is where we are meant to be."

It should be noted that the online dialogue is not always perfect. There are still the narrow-minded and the prejudiced. There are moments when I may not be clear enough on what I wish to express from my heart, moments when I will be hurt or accidentally hurt. But, in this world where safe spaces are so rare and kindred spirits so hard to locate, it has made all the difference.

I learned that there is no shame in wanting the best for humanity, in lowering yourself to your knees and supplicating a higher power to guide your heart. The studies I pursued in regard to my own religion and its roots—as well as within a university environment, focusing on liberal arts, classic traditions, and gender studies—confirmed to me that equality doesn't mean condemning and suppressing the right to individual decisions and self-expression, the right to choose what you believe in, or what clothes you wear.

The faith that had always been degraded as my shackles was, in fact, my wings.

Dear reader, regardless of what you believe, of what actions make you feel strong and confident and ready to empower yourself and reach out to others—your faith is not a weakness. It forms who you are, your hopes and your fears and your dreams for a better future. It is your experience, the fuel for your voice and the reason why you reach out to hear and boost other voices.

Our feminism rests in our faith. And there is nothing secondhand or shameful about that.

BECHDEL TEST

You might be familiar with the Bechdel Test (now called the Bechdel-Wallace test), especially if you're a movie fan. Named after comic artist Alison Bechdel, this simple test, which comes from her 1985 comic titled *Dykes to Watch Out For*, determines whether female characters in a movie, on TV, in books, or in other media are actively present with a value of their own or whether they exist for the sake of a male character alone. Media that pass the Bechdel-Wallace test do so by including at least two female characters who talk with each other about something other than a man.

In Search of Sisterhood

BY BRANDY COLBERT

"Do you wish you had sisters?"

I was surprised when my mom asked me that one day. I'd never thought much about it since I do have siblings—one older brother, and three younger from my dad's second marriage.

But my mom has six sisters from a family of thirteen children. The seven of them are spread out across three states, but they keep in touch so closely that to her, a life without sisters would drastically change things. They grew up sharing not only bedrooms but beds, and picked cotton together in my grandparents' fields when they were children. My mother has always lived a life infused with the friendship and sisterhood of black girls.

I, however, can count on one hand the number of black female friends I had as a child and teenager: two, if I include church friends.

I grew up in a predominantly white town in Missouri that was 3 percent black. A good portion of that percentage made up the membership of my black church, a small red-brick building with a baptismal pool hidden under the pulpit. There were kids my age who sat in the pews with their parents every Sunday, like me. We were crammed together at the front of the church for youth choir, practiced our parts in the Easter and Christmas programs, and attended Vacation Bible School together during the summer. But church friendships weren't the same as school friendships. My school friends I saw every day during the week, and with them I shared more with than a place of worship. But they weren't black.

I was friendly with the handful of black girls who went to my high school, but I wouldn't call us friends. We said hello in the hallways and classes we had together, but we didn't have the same interests or friend groups. "Friendly" was okay, but I wanted real black girlfriends I could confide in about the similarities that united us and the differences between us and our peers that we'd been taught to virtually ignore so we could fit in better. But the black-girlfriend void was nothing new, and I was used to it. After all, I was the only black girl at the dance studio I'd attended for seven years.

I felt appreciated and encouraged when I walked into that studio several times a week for hours of challenging tap and jazz classes, yet being there constantly reminded me how different I looked compared to everyone else. The "flesh-toned" tights we were all supposed to wear weren't anywhere close to the color of *my* skin. And while it seemed that so many of the girls were taking tap classes only to fill their dance package, tap dancing was my one true love. I always enjoyed watching ballet performances, but I never took lessons as a kid, and I wonder whether it was just my limited exposure to ballet that explained why I had never seen a black ballet dancer. There were no Misty Copelands or Michaela DePrinces to look up to back then, but the jazz and tap scene were different. Watching the immensely talented Gregory Hines and Savion Glover perform reinforced the love for tap that so few of my fellow white dancers seemed to share with me.

I hated that I was rarely in the company of people my age who looked like me when I was growing up. I felt as if I had to be the spokesperson for my race when I didn't yet understand the history behind being a black American myself. Black history instruction in school was limited to the month of February and the couple of days we talked about slavery, Jim Crow, and the civil rights movement. Those were some of the most uncomfortable days of my life.

My family had the Internet in the early 1990s, but online interaction was limited to chat rooms and forums, and there weren't websites where I could learn on my own about the black women who would later grow to mean a great deal to me, like civil rights activist Fannie Lou Hamer or Dorothy West, the Harlem Renaissance writer whom Langston Hughes nicknamed "the Kid." It seemed that the only black American deemed worthy enough for school discussion was Martin Luther King, Jr., whose words are often twisted today to justify widespread bigoted views.

Whenever anyone implies, or, even more foolishly, straight up declares that representation doesn't matter, I want to put them in my childhood shoes. Because I knew so few black girls my own age, I was starved for that representation in mainstream media—which consistently failed to deliver. Seeing so few faces like mine made me wonder what was wrong with girls who looked like me. I did regular, everyday things like the girls who were meant to speak for all teens, but it was rare to see black girls portrayed in a positive light. Allowing a group to exist only as stereotypes is an insidious type of erasure; I wanted to know that black girls mattered when we weren't just the subjects of harrowing news stories.

The movie *Clueless* was released a couple of months after I turned sixteen, and I bought a ticket to see it in the theater three times. It remains one of my favorite movies more than twenty years later, and part of that everlasting love is due to Dionne, who wore gorgeous box braids and a killer wardrobe and served as much more than the token black friend. Naturally I became obsessed with Brandy Norwood, who shared my name and birth year and whose eponymous CD case I'd stare at for long periods of time, in disbelief that a black girl with my name was singing on MTV and posing for magazine covers. And there is an entire section of my heart solely reserved for the members of TLC and Destiny's Child, whose legacies I will defend to the death.

The thing is, I had black women in my real life. In addition to my huge families on both my maternal and paternal sides, most of the women at my church had known me since a few weeks after I was born, and they were a fierce and loving group from several generations all gathered under one roof—one of my earliest examples of how varied black people are as a whole. I felt entirely included as we sang hymns together and when they called me Sister Colbert. I appreciate them more the older I get, but I've also realized that while it was important to have black women to look up to, it was just as important to have friendships with black girls my age.

Less than a month after college graduation, I packed up my things and moved across the country from Missouri to California. I was drawn to Los Angeles because of the perpetually warm temperatures and the abundance of palm trees, but after I'd been here awhile, my mother pointedly asked how many black people I was hanging out with. "Um, none?" I had to sheepishly admit. Because I'd been quite vocal about another reason I'd chosen LA: to meet a variety of people I wasn't exposed to in my hometown—including people who looked like me.

That finally changed a couple of years later when I was invited to hang out with a new group of people. My jaw might have actually scraped the floor when a girl named M showed up, sporting the same complexion and Valley Girl accent as yours truly; by the look on her face, she was just as surprised to see me. The only thing different about us seemed to be our hair—mine was newly natural while hers was relaxed.

I was raised in a household that celebrated black culture, from the dark-skinned dolls my parents must have painstakingly searched stores to find in the 1980s to the copies of *Jet* and *Ebony* they subscribed to for years. I knew black was beautiful, but I'd struggled with my hair for years, a feature that was inherently tied to my outer beauty and self-perception. And I didn't know *why* my gloriously thick hair had been pressed straight with a hot comb heated on the stove when I was a child, and then chemically relaxed into a limp, textureless imitation of my white classmates' bone-straight locks when I got older. I just knew that it seemed necessary to hide a certain part of me; showing my hair's natural coils would make a lot of people—even other black people—uncomfortable.

After twenty-two years with straightened or relaxed hair, I was tired of chemical burns on my scalp and avoiding raindrops and swimming pools. But I didn't know anyone in real life who had natural hair, and at the time, there were few resources that provided tutorials on how to transition, start dreadlocks, or execute the perfect twistout. Eventually, I stumbled onto a site with thousands of members from around the world, black women of all different shades, religions, sexualities, and socioeconomic backgrounds who were learning about and imparting their wisdom on black hair care.

That site has been invaluable, from teaching me the history behind the kinks of my hair to helping me find a family-owned business that sells products I still use more than a decade later. But maybe my best discovery was the woman around my age who made hair accessories by hand and was one of the funniest people I'd ever met online. We soon learned we were both fiction writers, aspiring to be published one day. Lesley is one of the most gifted writers I know, not least of all because her Nigerian American background is always at the root of her magical, breathtaking stories, and I don't think it's fair that she also has some of the most beautiful hair I've ever seen. I didn't realize at the time that she was becoming my first black female friend as an adult, but over ten years later, I feel incredibly lucky to count her as one of my most trusted friends.

While Lesley was thousands of miles away, M was there, in the flesh, in LA—a potential friend with whom I shared a background that we hadn't actually shared at all. We became fast friends after meeting, instantly bonding over experiences I'd assumed I'd never be able to discuss with someone else who truly understood. Like the fact that I'd been endlessly accused of "talking too white for a black girl," as if "talking white" is an actual existing thing. Or how, because of where we'd both grown up, we'd always had close friendships and relationships with white guys, which felt natural because we were connecting with other human beings, but also inherently wrong because of the history between black women and white men in this country, and the privilege they are afforded that we most certainly are not. M also shared my lack of friendships with other black women our age, which might have provided the most relief of all. I felt like I'd been searching for her my whole life, and when I said, "I thought I was the only person who grew up like that," she nodded and replied, "Me, too."

M and I remained close for a few years, and while we didn't end up having many common interests, our friendship allowed me to become more comfortable with who I was at the core. Because the truth was that I'd felt like a fraud for the better part of my life. While I was certainly black enough in the eyes of society, I'd heard numerous times that I wasn't *really* black. According to these upholders of blackness, I didn't talk or act black, and so I became self-conscious around groups of fellow black people, as if they'd accuse me of being the impostor I already suspected I was.

When church members called me Sister Colbert, I yearned to respond in kind with "Brother this" or "Sister that," but I was too afraid they'd see how hard it was for the words to roll off my tongue. As a writer, I struggled over crafting black characters, for fear that I would get the experience wrong; lack of representation made me believe there was only a handful of stories to tell, and that mine wouldn't make the cut. One of my biggest regrets, fueled by this overarching insecurity, was that I was too scared to pledge a black sorority in college. That would have been the ultimate sisterhood, and yet I was too worried that my blackness was inauthentic. I was convinced no one would ever see me as a true sister.

There was a long stretch of my twenties where I didn't have any black female friends who lived within a thousand miles, and I started to wonder if that was how it would always be.

I was working seriously toward publication around that time, and though I was nervous about my chances for success based on the lack of published novels about black teenage girls, I knew I had stories worth telling. And I began to realize that feeling so different from all of my friends when I was growing up wasn't something to be ashamed of, but to be shared. M and I couldn't have been the only girls who were raised in mostly white communities and felt self-conscious about our identities as black women.

So I wrote—three books that I eventually shelved, and one that became my debut novel.

I'm always happy when the book resonates with readers, but I'm especially proud when I hear from black girls and women who've connected with the story. It feels validating, but it also reminds me that no matter how different our lives are, we share the unique and fulfilling experience of having lived life as black women. And while publishing is still in dire need of more black women writers, I am so grateful to have found genuine, supportive friendship in the ones currently publishing alongside me.

Sometimes I've felt selfish for wanting more than what I've had. Because I've always surrounded myself with solid groups of friends who support me, and I certainly didn't choose them based on skin color. I have white friends who listen to me relay racist encounters and microaggressions without denying my experience. I have nonwhite friends who know what it's like to move through life feeling like the Other. But there is no substitute for a shared culture, no alternative for congregating with people whose roots belong to similar trees, and who understand the reasons behind the things you do without constantly having to ask for explanations.

Now I have more black female friends than ever before. And while I'll always wish there had been more representation of people who looked like me when I was a child and teen, I have an eternal soft spot for the black girls who repped for me back then, and it's empowering to see women like Lupita Nyong'o and Amandla Stenberg and Lena Waithe carry on that legacy with grace, humor, talent, and beauty.

I didn't grow up with the built-in network of sister-friends my mom had, but female friendships have always been an important part of my life. Finding friendship in women who understand what it's like to grow up both black and female has been essential to making me the strong and empathetic person I am today. And, ultimately, I've learned there is no key or special word for admittance into the black girls' club when you are a black girl.

So no, I don't wish for sisters and I never really have. As it turns out, black female friendships are good enough for me.

A Feminist Love

BY JESSICA LUTHER

I met him when I was still a kid. Or more accurately, I met him just after I had graduated from being a kid, only a few months past my eighteenth birthday. He was cute, shy, smart, and kind.

I was sitting in the lounge of my college dorm, pretending to be a studious freshman, my astronomy textbook open to a page about solar flares. I could not tell you what a solar flare is now, but I know that's what I was reading the day I met my husband. (It's one of those visceral memories that has stayed with me.) My eyes returned to the picture again and again as I spent many minutes sneaking glances at the boy just over there, the one I hoped was noticing me, too. My body was warm, flushed just from his being near. That feeling of warmth would become familiar to me; I still get it when he's around.

I have been with that boy, now a nearly middle-aged man, for almost half my life. Our relationship is my most successful accomplishment.

Pop culture has a pretty strong message about what love and relationships should look like: two people, white, heterosexual, monogamous, unending, happy, easy. Most romantic comedies are based on this formula, as are the majority of romance novels. The foundation for these relationships is always love. *Love conquers all. All you need is love. I'm just a girl standing in front of a boy, asking him to love her.* After all, this isn't sixteenth-century Europe where everyone was poor and barely subsisting, where marriage, for most people, was not a choice but a means of survival. Now we choose our partners and stay with them primarily out of love. Or so we say.

At the same time, we have strong messages about how women should act. Women are often taught—or outright told—to prioritize everyone's feelings, needs, and desires over and above their own. Women are supposed to sacrifice their own happiness for the larger stability of their marriage or their family with rarely a call for the other person in the relationship to do the same. They may remain silent in the face of abuse and loss of personal identity, and be praised for it.

A feminist relationship rejects this notion. In a feminist relationship, all parties should have equal standing when it comes to whose feelings are honored, whose needs are met first, and whose desires are prioritized. That is a feminist love.

It's tricky, though. From the outside, a heterosexual relationship may not look like a feminist relationship; it may appear to be based on regular old patriarchy (man in control of woman and the relationship). At times, the feelings, needs, and desires of a man in a relationship may trump another person's. At other times, a woman in a relationship may make a decision to participate in activities stereotyped as "the things women do": primary caregiver for a child, main household chore completer, or maker of dinners. Sometimes you are going to *like* the tropes in romantic comedies and romance novels that people may tell you are un-feminist to like or want. That's okay.

But here's a secret to the feminist relationship: the current state of a relationship is always temporary. Perhaps your partner's needs are being met first today, or this week, or even this year. If you are in a feminist relationship, you know that when the time comes—when you *need*—things will change. And you are, most of the time, okay with that compromise. That is a feminist love.

I got married when I was twenty-two. At that point, I had been with my husband for nearly four and a half years. We had already been to couples counseling and survived a cross-country move. And throughout the last seventeen years together, we have allowed each other to grow as individuals while always allowing space for our relationship to grow, too. We are not the same kids who met in college, or the same people who moved across the country post-graduation, or even the same people who became parents seven years ago. Just like our relationship, we, as people, are always changing. For my husband and me, acknowledging the ever-changing aspects of ourselves and our relationship is a big part of how we manage. We deliberately make time for each other in the midst of chaotic days, jobs, parenting, and a host of other obligations. We recognize that we are not perfect, our relationship certainly isn't, our communication skills need work, and we are lucky to have found each other. No matter how quickly I've turned a corner, he's never let go of my hand, even if sometimes our arms get stretched as far as they can go.

I can't imagine any point when I would want to not be a part of this relationship. But I do think I'll know if that moment ever comes. It will be the point when my individual identity is lost completely, and I don't recognize myself except as part of this relationship, or when the same happens to him (though the odds of the latter are less likely, given our social programming in this land of men). Or when one of us has monopolized everything in the relationship and prioritization of the other person does not seem possible. Or when one of us injures the other irreparably. I'm optimistic these things won't happen, but I allow space to imagine them so I'll recognize them if they do. I think that, too, is part of a feminist love.

Relationships don't always look like mine, and they shouldn't; that's the point. For some people, the best relationship is one where they are the only individual in it, where it is solely about what they want or need without ever having to negotiate with someone else. For others, it's a relationship that isn't one-to-one, but allows for multiple partners and commitments. Or it's a couple without children or a couple with ten kids. These are all feminist loves, too.

So, seventeen years into this relationship and thirty-five years into my life, I can't tell you that love is always grand. It can be, and when it is, hold on to it. When love stops being grand, though, accept it and move on. I would also never say that love is easy. If you are going to try at love, you've got to know it takes work before you even start. Nor will I tell you that it's enough to find someone who, when you're around them, makes you like yourself more and brings out the best things you knew were inside you but couldn't quite access. Love is not enough on its own if you want to be a complete person living a complete life. There has to be more to it than that. There has to be more to *you* than that. Embrace a feminist love inside a relationship, but never forget to embrace a feminist love of yourself.

Here is what I can tell you about love: it is warm. There is a literal sense to this: a warm body that hugs you when you are sad, that hugs you when you succeed, that snuggles against you in bed when you're cold, that holds your hand when you go to the doctor to manage your mental illness, that holds your hand and breathes alongside you as you push a baby into the world, that holds your hand because being next to someone is a reminder that you are not alone. But love's warmth is also metaphorical. It is that feeling of confidence that envelops you when you are sitting across the table from a potential employer in a job interview, that feeling of comfort because you know someone in your life sees you as you want to be seen, that feeling of joy when you finally complete a long project and know that someone will be as happy for you as you are for yourself. This is how love operates in my life and my relationship, and that warmth has never gone away.

I wish that, in whatever form, you find that wonderful feminist love and that it keeps you warm.

CHAPTER six

CONFIDENCE and AMBITION

It can be
RADICAL

to have confidence, ambition, bravery, and boldness in a world like the one we live in.

Women who are leaders in their professions, like New York Times former executive editor Jill Abramson or political powerhouse Hillary Clinton, are called "pushy," "brusque," "manly," or "bossy" in mainstream media because they're unwilling to fit a narrow mold of what is and isn't acceptable female behavior and ambition.

It's not just women who are subjected to these standards. While men may be praised for their leadership skills in ways that females are not, those who choose not to be leaders may be labeled as weak, feminine, sensitive, or otherwise defective, even if those same men are perfectly content in who they are.

There's no shame in being strong, and there's no one way to be strong. Strength is about being true to yourself and your values. Being a feminist means being both confident and ambitious in your day-to-day life as well as bold and brave in big ways that stretch you outside your comfort zone.

Take ownership and pride in the things that make you who you are and who you want to be.

The "Nice Girl" Feminist

BY ASHLEY HOPE PÉREZ

I grew up in a conservative community in East Texas, smack in the middle of the Bible Belt. I learned the Ten Commandments before I lost my first tooth. It wasn't until I was older, though, that I was able to see other rules that had governed my girlhood and adolescence, mostly without me ever noticing. For these commandments, there were no impressive stone tablets, no Moses, no Mount Sinai. What I think of now as "the Nice Girl Commandments" were communicated subtly through daily interactions at home, school, church, and work.

Like anyone else, "nice girls" can become feminists. But here's the thing: I *do* think that we "nice girls" have to learn to see the almost-invisible rules that we've been socialized to live by. We also have to understand how those rules have shaped what we do and say. And *then* we can begin to break the "commandments" that make it hard for us to be ourselves—and therefore to attain our full potential. Here are the top four "nice girl" commandments that I had to break on my way to feminism. Yours might be very different, and that's okay! But don't let your actions—big or small—be bound by rules with inequality at their core.

COMMANDMENT # 1: NICE GIRLS DO NOT TALK BACK.

Most people think of "talking back" as a mark of bad behavior or disrespect that unfolds like this: a grown-up—usually a parent or teacher—gives an instruction or makes a request, and instead of doing what's asked, a girl asks why, objects, or otherwise expresses resistance. It's probably best to speak respectfully to parents and people in charge, but for young women in the South, even the most thoughtfully framed questions or objections can get taken as "lip" or talking back. Whereas it's expected that men will voice their opinions and advocate for their interests, young women are often trained to stay mild and sweet even in the face of comments that are inappropriate or problematic.

Once, when I was a teenager eating out with my family, an older man from church walked by our table, patted my head, and called me a "pretty little thing." He smiled and lingered for a moment, waiting for my response. I knew that I was supposed to smile graciously and say thank you. I didn't do that—I think my grandmother finally said something pleasant to fill the silence—but I also didn't say what I was thinking. *Because nice girls don't talk back.* I knew I was not supposed to point out that, as a seventeen-year-old woman, I was neither "little" nor a "thing." I was not supposed to say that I'd rather be complimented on my intellect than on my appearance.

During college, I began talking back. Not a lot. But sometimes. When the pastor of the church I attended told me that women could lead only the children's Bible studies, I asked why. When my mom asked me to help clean up the dishes after a big Thanksgiving family gathering, I agreed, but I also pointed out that my brother should be helping, too. And just this year, when a hospital administrator insisted that the accent mark in my family's name couldn't be put on our son's birth certificate, I explained why it was important and asked, respectfully but firmly, to speak to someone who might be able to help us resolve the problem.

Over the fifteen years since I moved away from East Texas, talking back—respectfully, thoughtfully, with a willingness to listen—has become part of my repertoire of adult actions. I think that, even now, it sometimes surprises people when I talk back, because I still give off that "nice girl" vibe.

But I like keeping them on their toes.

COMMANDMENT #2: NICE GIRLS DON'T MEDDLE.

On the surface, this might seem not all that different from the injunction against talking back. But the "no meddling" rule has more to do with keeping comments to yourself when you hear or see something, especially when the situation doesn't seem to be your business. One of the great evils of Southern discretion, in my opinion, is how it's been used to justify turning a blind eye to situations that need serious redress. There's a reason that we had to write laws making it a crime *not* to report suspected child abuse, for example.

I remember my own feeling of paralysis when a friend and I ran into her house to get something, and I heard her cousin at the back of the house shouting at his girlfriend in a way I'm pretty sure he wouldn't have if he'd known we were there. His tone was nastier than anything I'd ever heard from an adult, and his girlfriend sounded scared. Their baby started crying, and his shouting got louder. My friend and I looked at each other for a long moment, and then we ran out of the house. We never talked about it. Looking back, I'd say the situation pointed toward verbal abuse; even then, I knew something was wrong, but the "nice girl" code kept us quiet.

Since then, little by little, I've learned to reframe "meddling" in ways that help me take action when the "nice girl" in me wants to step back. Often, I think of it as making people aware that someone has noticed what is happening. If I'm in a store and an employee is rude to a Spanish-speaking customer whose English is limited, I make a point of helping the customer—and of asking for the employee's name. When I see a manager, I let him or her know what I saw and emphasize that it's a problem for any customer to be treated with disrespect.

It can also help to think about getting involved as a kind of advocacy. In my days teaching high school in Houston, I taught a number of young women who had babies or who were pregnant. It might not have been the path I would have chosen for these students, but I felt strongly that their family situation or reproductive circumstances shouldn't change my expectations for them. If I happened to walk through the teachers' lounge and heard someone airing their negativity about "those girls" or suggesting that they wouldn't amount to anything, I put myself right in that teacher's business. My approach was usually to highlight the accomplishments of a pregnant student we had in common or to ask the bad-mouther what I could do to help the student be more successful in that teacher's class. Maybe my "meddling" words did little to change the teacher's private view, but at least I identified myself as an advocate for the student.

You don't have to make some big stand to intervene meaningfully. You know that moment when you walk into a public restroom and hear someone crying in a stall? (By the way, I've *been* that crying woman plenty of times.) You hurt for that person, but, at the same time, you kind of wish you could just run out of the bathroom and "unhear" the crying. Do you mind your business or get involved? A fear of meddling has held me back in the past, but I've come to realize that my discomfort matters a lot less than the possibility—however distant—that a word or two of concern might help. You can ask gentle questions: "Do you need to talk to someone?" "Can I help you get somewhere?" If nothing else, the chica knows that her pain wasn't ignored. What might look like meddling to some can in fact be an act of solidarity and simple human kindness.

COMMANDMENT #3: NICE GIRLS SHOULD BE PRETTY BUT *NEVER* SEXUAL.

Curl your eyelashes, put on your makeup, straighten your hair, strap on a padded bra, lie down on the bed to squeeze into your jeans; whatever it takes to look good. In the East Texas I knew growing up, nice girls didn't wear anything too revealing, but it was still important to make an effort to be appealing. A nice girl should be pretty, even sexy, but not, of course, S-L-U-T-T-Y. It was fine to be desirable so long as you made sure not to have any desires of your own. Because the boundary between "sexy" and "slutty" was all about desire. The idea was that "bad" girls wanted to do it and therefore did it too much, whereas "nice" girls weren't supposed to be or want to be sexual. Ever.

I remember when everything changed for me. It was long, long before I actually had sex. Somebody at my college was doing a survey and asked if I'd had an orgasm. It was the first time I'd heard the word spoken aloud. I turned beet red and said, from the depth of my nice-girl self, "No, of course not!" I assumed that this was the right answer; and it was technically true at the time. But my interviewer couldn't disguise her dismay. "Never?" she asked, just to make sure.

"Never," I said, but this time I understood that she thought I was missing out, and I made a mental note that will probably seem hilarious to people who grew up in more sexually open places: *Find out what the big deal about orgasms is.* I'd been aroused before, but until that moment, I didn't realize that I should feel anything but shame about the experience.

In the same year as the survey, I saw *The Vagina Monologues.* To say the names of things was another step toward liberation: vagina, penis, orgasm, pubic hair. I blushed but vowed not to tiptoe around sexual realities anymore.

A few years later, my boyfriend and I had sex. Very awkward sex. (It did get better, though.) Afterward, I thought about all the places in the world where I would now be considered a "bad" girl as well as all the places where I was still a "nice" girl. And then I thought most about those places—including the bedroom I was in—where having sex really didn't say anything about me one way or the other.

COMMANDMENT # 4: NICE GIRLS ALWAYS SMILE.

And finally . . . the commandment that was most painful for me to uphold and that, ironically, has also been the hardest for me to break. When I tell people where I'm from, I sometimes get comments like, "Oh my gosh, I went to Dallas once, and people were so friendly, it was *creepy*." I remember how, shortly after I moved to Massachusetts for my first year of college, I went to my dorm room and cried after a gas station clerk just stared at me when I said, "Hi, how are you?" Greeting people who pass you on the sidewalk or in the grocery store is just what you *do* in the South; it's one of those unspoken rules that you follow.

Another unspoken rule is that everyone must declare the sunniness of life in these interactions. No one *actually* wants to know how you are; it's a courtesy that creates a space for you to smile and say, "I'm good, thanks!" or at least, "I'm fine. How are you?" Nice girls, even more than anyone else, are expected to be sunny, cheerful, smiling, and always "Great!"

What harm is there in a smile? Plenty. Especially if you're trying to be a nice girl when your grandmother has cancer or when you don't know how your family will pay the bills or when things are otherwise not okay. It feels awful to keep doing the sunshine routine when it feels like your world is falling apart. You smile and you smile and you smile—and all the while you feel how ridiculously divided your inner experience is from what you can show to anyone. And you don't know how to bridge the gap.

When I was fifteen, I went through this kind of performance for months after my mother attempted suicide. And if the scariness of the situation made me feel alone, pretending I was fine made that feeling a hundred times worse. The same thing was true when I suffered a serious bout of depression yet kept on smiling. As I went through treatment, I vowed that I would never again paste a smile over my experience of the world. I knew I had to find a way to answer even casual inquiries with some measure of honesty.

Don't get me wrong; it's not like I now unpack my grimmest baggage for every person who asks me how I'm doing. But if I don't feel happy, I try not to fake it. I say, "I'm getting by," "Tomorrow will be better," or "You know how it goes." Someone who really wants to know what's up with me will ask more; someone who doesn't will just let it go. This may seem small, but it's a surprisingly powerful form of honesty. Best of all, you don't have to have everything figured out to give yourself the right to say how you really are.

THE "NICE GIRL" FEMINIST

I wouldn't be surprised if readers raised in more liberal communities are belly laughing by now at the earnestness of my struggle to overcome the burden of niceness. *Who worries about this stuff?* they might wonder. But some of you know exactly what I'm talking about. And part of the journey to feminism is discovering that what felt to us like commandments were really just the norms of our community.

These days, I identify with generosity and hope (it is my middle name, after all) rather than the blander, potentially conformity-inducing ideal of "niceness" that still prevails in much of the South. There may be a fundamental conflict between feminism and striving to be somebody else's idea of a "nice girl," but feminism is perfectly compatible with genuine warmth, optimism, and courtesy. In fact, these characteristics—often associated with "niceness"—can help the cause of feminism.

For all the work I put into breaking free from "nice girl" expectations, knowing how to navigate interactions with folks expecting a "nice girl" helps me bring feminism to those who might not be receptive to my more militant friends. I'm not suggesting that everyone should adopt my style; we need women who speak the truth bluntly and without reservation. Still, my softer approach improves the chances that some people—my grandfather, for example—will think about what I'm saying instead of recoiling reflexively from feminism. And if my "nice girl" legacy gives important ideas a footing in a handful of conversations, I'll count myself lucky to have had my particular journey to feminism.

The "nice girl" standard is riddled with contradictions. Once you see them, you realize that you don't have to live up to anybody else's idea of what to be or how to act moment by moment. Ditching the "nice girl" game is, itself, a feminist act.

5 TIPS FOR "NICE GIRL" FEMINISTS:

#1 Be nice to yourself. Resist any nasty or super-critical inner monologues. Talk to yourself like you'd talk to a friend.

#2 Trust your intuition & say what you think — even if it might make someone uncomfortable. Discomfort can be a step toward change.

#3 Don't hide behind a mask of niceness. Your friends — and your friendships — can handle your real feelings.

#4 Don't worry about how you come across. Even when you think you are being a "bad girl" feminist, chances are that you will still seem pretty nice.

#5 Be patient with yourself. Getting over being a "nice girl" is a process.

¡ XOXO y abrazos!

Ashley Hope Pérez

P.S. That is a butterfly, in case you can't tell. "Nice girl" me was the caterpillar. Feminist me is the butterfly. **No regrets!**

Ashley Hope Pérez

Shrinking Women

BY LILY MYERS

Across from me at the kitchen table,
    my mother smiles over red wine that
    she drinks out of a measuring glass.

She says she doesn't deprive herself,

but I've learned to find nuance in every
    movement of her fork.

In every crinkle in her brow as she
    offers me the uneaten pieces on
    her plate.

I've realized she only eats dinner when
    I suggest it.

I wonder what she does when I'm not
    there to do so.

Maybe this is why my house feels
    bigger each time I return; it's
    proportional.

As she shrinks, the space around her
    seems increasingly vast.

She wanes while my father waxes. His
    stomach has grown round with
    wine, late nights, oysters, poetry. A
    new girlfriend who was overweight
    as a teenager, but my dad reports
    that now she's "crazy about fruit."

It was the same with his parents;

as my grandmother became frail and
    angular, her husband swelled to
    red round cheeks, rotund stomach,

and I wonder if my lineage is one of
    women shrinking,

making space for the entrance of men
    into their lives,

not knowing how to fill it back up once
    they leave.

I have been taught accommodation.

My brother never thinks before he
    speaks.

I have been taught to filter.

"How can anyone have a relationship
    to food?" he asks, laughing, as I eat
    the black bean soup I chose for its
    lack of carbs.

I want to say: We come from differ-
    ence, Jonas.

You have been taught to grow out;

I have been taught to grow in.

You learned from our father how to emit, how to produce, to roll each thought off your tongue with confidence; you used to lose your voice every other week from shouting so much.

I learned to absorb.

I took lessons from our mother in creating space around myself.

I learned to read the knots in her forehead while the guys went out for oysters

and I never meant to replicate her, but

spend enough time sitting across from someone and you pick up their habits.

That's why women in my family have been shrinking for decades.

We all learned it from one another, the way each generation taught the next how to knit,

weaving silence in between the threads,

which I can still feel as I walk through this ever-growing house,

skin itching,

picking up all the habits my mother has unwittingly dropped like bits of crumpled paper from her pocket on her countless trips from bedroom to kitchen to bedroom again,

nights I hear her creep down to eat plain yogurt in the dark, a fugitive stealing calories to which she does not feel entitled.

Deciding how many bites are too many

how much space she deserves to occupy.

Watching the struggle, I either mimic or hate her,

and I don't want to do either anymore,

but the burden of this house has followed me across the country.

I asked five questions in genetics class today and all of them started with the word "sorry."

I don't know the capstone requirements for the sociology major because I spent the entire meeting deciding whether or not I could have another piece of pizza

a circular obsession I never wanted but

inheritance is accidental

still staring at me with wine-stained lips from across the kitchen table.

Dear Teen Me: It Would Have Changed Everything; It Would Have Changed Nothing

BY ERIKA T. WURTH

Dear sixteen-year-old Erika,

I write this letter a lot to you in my head, over and over. Often before I go to sleep. Because I'm one of those people who occasionally like to delude myself into thinking that if I'd only known things before I experienced them, I could have changed what came after.

LOL, as they say now. Because I was born in 1975 and was a grumpy loner who ate lunch under the display case to avoid the mullets beating me up for reading dragon books, when I hear this phrase, it sounds to me like a prom queen screaming.

Like every kid back then, white, Native American, or Latina, if you were alive in the 1980s, you permed your hair. Damn right you did. And if you didn't have blond hair, often, you made sure that you did. So, though my hair was slowly becoming thick, straight, and dark (my hair had been light when I was very young), my mom and I felt it better to make it the opposite. Since my hair was thick, this made it very very large, sort of like a big blond-orange "Arnold from Different Strokes" fro. Looking back on it, this did not stop me from being a weirdo who liked to read dragon books, did not have a kid, or a mullet, and was honestly, kind of wussy.

That made my mom sad. But it turned out okay. Though that's the thing: like I said, often I think that things would be different if I could go back in time and tell myself how it's going to be like now. That the immense loneliness wouldn't go away, but that it would be easier to bear, that in many ways, it's what I need, who I am. That dragon books are cool, but that they were just not going to be the thing I was going to write, and God knows why. That I would never get a boyfriend (because this was and is the standard for normal), but I would be spared so many things that I could not have born, like hating the person beside me. That somehow if I could go back in time and tell myself that being a writer was okay, that despite whatever everyone said, that not only could a nerdy Native chick become a writer, but a nerdy Native chick could become a creative writing professor, and that would give me so much time to write, and that it would be something I would be very lucky to get even if it put me in tremendous debt. That my parents were wrong: I would never "write on the side," whatever that meant to them, and me.

The problem is that sometimes I think that if I could go and tell myself these things, that I would be living in a city, not a small midwestern town where strangers touch my hair. That I would have a boyfriend, a cool Native nerd like me, and we'd have cool Native nerd babies. That I would have gotten that book out when I was thirty, not thirty-nine, and that somehow me and my Native dude and our adorable Native kids would be living some kind of miracle life in let's say, Albuquerque. But that's a lie. And it's a boring, selfish one, because I have so much. I have everything.

I have it all because even though I desperately wanted to be a writer (whatever that means when you're twelve years old, staring at the author photo on the back of a dragon book around two a.m. because of insomnia), in all honesty, I thought I wouldn't be brave enough to be one. Underneath it all, no matter how much I fought my mom's friends when they told me I should teach elementary school because of how well I do with kids (and honestly because I was a girl, and honestly because I was a Native girl), I thought that I wouldn't make it. And sometimes I tell myself (truthfully, all the time) that if I'd just become something else, I would at least live in a city where strangers don't touch my hair. And I wish that were true often, because when you talk about the things I talk about, you are called vulgar, you are called dark, you are called bleak, you are called all kinds of things in reviews and to your face and by presses and publishers that are spiritually diminishing.

It used to be when I looked at Burroughs' fantastical representation of his typewriter as a cockroach crossed with an asshole, I'd laugh. Laugh because, honestly, that image is funny. But laugh also because it seemed so self-indulgent. Like, really, dude? You get to be a writer, that's the best thing in the world, shut up. You could *choose* to be something else. But that was before I realized that no, he couldn't have, and that there is so little romance in that statement. Before more than a decade of being told that my work is dark, vulgar, before I realized that I would live, off and on for a decade, in a place where strangers touch my hair. Before I realized that the writing would take everything, that I would choose it before everything else, without even knowing that I was doing it.

But that doesn't change the fact that no matter what people call me and my work, the one thing that they *have* to call me is writer. And that is something that, had I been able to tell myself at sixteen, would have filled me with something so intangibly beautiful that it would have changed everything, it would have changed nothing, it would have made all the difference in the world.

THIS PIECE WAS PREVIOUSLY PUBLISHED ON *DEAR TEEN ME,* DEARTEENME.COM.

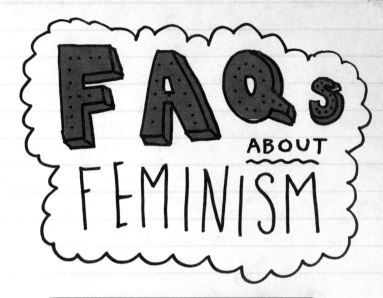

FAQs ABOUT FEMINISM

If sexism is being prejudiced against someone because of their sex, can women be sexist toward men?

By definition, sexism is discrimination against someone based on their gender. It's not that simple, though, as sexism against men in a society that favors men does not *harm* them in the same way that it does women or nonconforming individuals. This power imbalance matters: sexism actively hurts those who are not benefitting from social advantages. Feminists don't believe women can be sexist toward men, because men do not experience prejudice or discrimination in our society. Women can, however, be sexist toward nonconforming individuals, and they can be transphobic (actively harmful and prejudiced against trans individuals).

Isn't it sexist to point out gender?

This is a strange but common question. It's not sexist to point out gender. Part of intersectional feminism is understanding the ways gender collides with social norms or expectations and how that impacts an individual. It's worth talking about gender, since it is a part of one's identity that can be constantly in flux.

A Thousand Paper Cuts

BY SHVETA THAKRAR

Once upon a time, there was a girl who forgot she had a voice.

You know that feeling when you walk around in your body and it feels too tight, too itchy, too strange, and you can't relax because an ogre named Anxiety set up house in your chest? When every time your heart beats, Anxiety extracts a toll, as if it's the landlord and you're the tenant? When you put yourself on the page, but it will never be good enough for anyone else, when your raw, bloody heart's smashed into letters and words and paragraphs—can't they see the gore still dripping? What more do they *want*?—and none of it matters?

Besides, everyone knows girls are meant to be seen, not heard.

I know that pain. All the ways people deny you, try to correct and change you, are like a thousand tiny paper cuts. Even now, they're etched into my skin, scars only I can see.

How do you become a writer if you can't own your own words?

Once upon a time, there was a girl whose skin bled from too many incisions to count.

I remember being thirteen, fourteen, fifteen, and daydreaming so vividly, I could feel it in every single cell: my crushes would like me back; I'd be invited into the groups at school; I could be a writer. I even sent the first chapter of a Forgotten Realms novel to the publisher and waited for my contract.

None of those dreams came true, not one. The same boys who inspired butterfly ballets in my stomach weren't shy about calling me stupid and ugly and mocking my brown skin—one cut. Those groups of friends I yearned to be part of threw things in my hair and left me out of their parties—another cut. At least the publisher took the time to send a personal rejection, though that "no" just felt like one more wound.

Yet I never stopped wanting. I only stopped believing I could *have* what I wanted.

Get sliced open enough, bleed enough, and you start to hold back. You ball yourself up tight, so there's less of you showing.

Our world makes sure we know that girls don't get to have things, that we must confine ourselves to the roles pushed on us from outside, with labels like polite, subservient, and compliant. We're judged by how feminine we are, ridiculed for that same femininity (or lack of it), and have our ideas and insights minimized or credited to men. Do we look right (are we slender, conventionally pretty, white)? Do we sound right (are we soft-spoken)? Do we apologize for existing and retreat when challenged (because only difficult people take up space)? It's so much easier just to follow the path everyone else says we should.

For a long time, I did that. I folded myself up, ignored my heart's assertion that I was an artist, a philosopher who had things to say about her world. I had tales to tell, imagination in perpetual bloom, yet I crushed them in favor of pleasing others. I knew no one wanted my dreams.

Inside, though, I withered, growing depressed. And still those stories pushed against my insides, clamoring to be told.

Ambition is hard to have. We get told to lean in, that we're too soft and sensitive—because showing emotion is a punishable act in a patriarchal world—yet if we act "tough," we're derided as "ballbusters" and "bitches" and reminded our job is to smile for the men and make them a sandwich.

But that's slowly changing with each one of us who speaks up and out, who forges her own path.

Daring to want something and going after it is a feminist act. It's stating that you put your faith in your own intuition over what others tell you, and if you make mistakes along the way, you'll handle them. When you're ambitious, you want to do something, and that very act reshapes the world.

You cast open doors for those who come after you. Sometimes that means smashing down entire walls.

(Well-behaved ladies rarely make history.)

Once upon a time, there was a girl who swam through a sea of magic and longed to share its waters with the world.

In my early twenties, I looked at my library and noticed no one was putting out the fantasy literature I'd always hungered for, tales of South Asian mythical beings and characters with brown skin and names like mine. Someone needed to fix that.

Maybe, I thought, my heart fluttering hummingbird quick with doubts, then dreams, then doubts again, maybe *I* could be that someone.

Still doubting, still dreaming, I wrote my first story since I was a teenager—and walked right into a flood of dismissive comments. "What you're doing is niche." "Brown people don't sell." "Sure, we'll take your food and your yoga and your Bollywood movies, but you can't expect us to read a book about you."

I dared to get ambitious, and some people—many people—told me I was silly. That what I was doing, my writing and speaking, didn't count. That the bits of me smeared on the page, dripping with my desires, my wishes, my experiences as an Indian American girl, were "unrelatable."

They might as well have said, "This is our playground. You don't belong here, brown girl."

I've always been a feminist, someone who knew women and men (and nonbinary people) were equal. At some point, however, I realized misogyny—the way our culture teaches us to loathe and shame women while viewing them as less than men—wasn't the whole picture. There were many other modes of keeping people marginalized or shut down, methods like insisting you didn't matter if you weren't white. If you weren't straight. If you weren't Christian. If you weren't able-bodied and neurotypical. If you weren't at least middle class. If you weren't cisgender. If you weren't thin.

What about all the girls who weren't those things? What about *me*?

I didn't yet know how to believe in myself, how to revive my old dreams, but I did know no single group had a lock on the world. That was when I found third-wave feminism, which understood intersectionality—the fact that oppression happens on multiple fronts—and embraced the idea that all women—all *people*—matter.

Our voices matter, all of them. Our stories need to be told. And so I kept writing.

I wanted to see my thoughts and dreams made real. I wanted to see everyone's thoughts and dreams made real. I wanted to see everyone's art, their plans for our future. Your plans, whatever your background and experience. I still do.

I kept writing, I sold my stories, and I'm here to tell you the playground belongs to *all* of us.

Once upon a time, there was a girl who suspected she was part monster—and might have been proud of that.

Unfortunately, everyone else had their own thoughts on the subject: I was ugly; I was stupid; I was too brown; I wasn't brown enough; I was too loud and opinionated; I was too meek and didn't stand up for myself enough; my passions (reading, daydreaming, writing, fantasy and folklore) were meaningless. So I quit. I quit drawing; I quit writing; I quit talking.

But here's the thing: other people's opinions are not the truth. We live in a world that puts us into boxes and labels them with Sharpies, yet those boxes are lies. They flatten us; they limit who we really are.

Feminism is about flattening the *boxes* instead and tossing them out with the recycling. Who says a black girl can't beam at us from the cover of a best-selling book? That a South Asian girl can't grace the American twenty-dollar bill? That a blond white girl can't fly commercial jets? That a queer girl can't invent a self-sustaining fuel source? We're the only ones who can determine what labels we'll accept, if any.

It took me years to throw off my mantle of self-loathing, to be able to look in the mirror and claim my brown skin and my strange way of seeing the world, to be able to love them, even, but I did it. I did it because it finally became clear that the way I thought, the things I believed and felt, and my vision for my life were the things that gave me my power.

They were also the things that let me make my mark.

Sharing yourself, your thoughts, your aspirations, is a feminist act. Our world tells us both in subtle ways and with sapphirine neon signs how irrelevant we are, that no contribution we make can really matter in the long run. That goes triply if those girls are girls of color or queer or disabled or anything else society has deemed doesn't count.

Except you don't have to listen. You can set your own goals and trust yourself to know your worth. You can choose to jump right out of those boxes and write your own narrative.

At its core, feminism is about reclaiming your voice and helping others do the same. It's about embracing the parts of you the world considers monstrous, the parts that shine with the radiance only you have—your power, your beauty, your passion, your story.

After all, a single flame may light innumerable candles.

Once upon a time, there was a girl who unfurled her wings and reveled in her strong serpentine tail.

You don't need me to tell you the world isn't kind to girls. You experience it every day. There will be people who try to stop you, who demand you be less than you are, and maybe they'll sound like they're right, and you should back down.

I disagree. As a human being, you have a place in the world. If you have a place in the world, you matter. If you matter, so do other people, even if their experiences are completely unlike yours. Even if you don't like them. Feminism is about making sure everyone has a seat at the table that is life on Earth.

Feminism is about having compassion, for others and for ourselves. It's about living in our bodies and owning them. It's about going after the things we want and believing—knowing—the world needs our voices, our vision.

Your dynamic, beating heart, whether you share it through art or sports or science or activism or celebrating your heritage or whatever else you love, that eager, pounding heart is exactly what we all need. I hear it thrumming with your vitality, with the sheer power you're beginning to tap into, and it leaves my mouth dry with awe. I wonder how it will mold our culture.

I can't wait to see.

Once upon a time, there was a girl who found her voice again.

She'd channeled her unwelcome lodger Anxiety into Empathy. She'd learned the value of her worldview. Now it was time to speak.

She spoke and she spoke and she spoke, about misogyny and racism, about being a brown girl who loved fantasy but never saw herself in books, about magic and compassion and writing. To her shock, people listened. They read her stories. "I never thought of that!" they said. "Do you have any ideas for how can we do better?"

Well, thought the girl, who actually had many, many ideas, *if this is what happens when I speak up, just me, what would it be like to have all the girls in the world blossom petal and pistil into who they are, no holding back? Instead, they just go for what they want and, in doing so, extend a hand to other girls, too?*

She decided to find out.

Dear reader, I'm holding out my hand to you. Are you ready to jump?

The Win That Comes from Losing

BY WENDY DAVIS

On the morning of November 5, 2014—the morning after the biggest and most public "fail" I have ever had—I pulled myself out of my hotel-suite bed, and prepared to go to my Texas gubernatorial campaign headquarters for the last time. Fifty or so of the most vital members of my team, people who had worked tirelessly for the past year, would be gathered there. *What will I say to them?* I wondered. We had come together, believing with our whole hearts in what we were working to achieve: restoring the voice of real people to the Texas capitol. And each of us was suffering from the deep disappointment of the previous day's loss.

I had been in this hotel suite before. It was in 2008, the night I won my long-shot race to be elected as a Texas state senator in what had been considered a safe Republican seat. The suite, at the former historic Hotel Texas, was the one in which President John F. Kennedy spent his final night before heading to Dallas on that fateful morning in 1963. Staying there was meaningful to me; the hotel was both a piece of American history and the site of my greatest political triumph.

How different the morning following my victorious senate election had been! In 2008, I woke up filled with happy adrenaline. In 2014, I suffered the dull thud of a headache, and the beginnings of a heartache. Picking through the mostly uneaten food still spread out on the dining table, I found an empty wineglass, filled it with warm champagne, and took a shot for courage. I pulled on a pair of jeans and headed to the lobby for the drive over to my campaign headquarters on Fort Worth's south side.

The mood was somber when I walked into the large, dark, windowless, wood-paneled conference room. Not yet knowing what I was going to say, I opened my mouth and something from the most honest part of me tumbled out: "I fucking hate to lose."

I had been raised that way. Not to swear, but to be driven to compete. My father had a love for games of every sort. And, unlike parents who let their kids beat them, my dad played to win. In doing so, he pushed us to do our best. I'll never forget his glee when he'd thwack my croquet ball off course on his way to a win; nor the proud look on his face the first time I beat him in a chess match. In each competition, my dad sought to teach us the value of being gracious in both victory and defeat. But, man oh man, was winning better.

I credit the competitive spirit I learned from my dad as my driving force. It's what helped me scramble out of poverty as a young single mom and put myself on a better path. From the trailer where I once lived with my young daughter, Amber, to community college, and ultimately, to Harvard Law School, the fight he instilled in me got me through some tough times. That desire to always do more, to be my best self at whatever challenge came my way—I wouldn't be who I am without it.

My journey has taught me that, while it's easy to see the value of success in winning, tremendous benefits also come from the work involved in losing. Because there is value in fighting for something important to you, even when the outcome is not what you hoped it would be.

Have you ever seen that quote from American pastor Robert Schuller, "What is the one thing you would attempt if you knew you could not fail?" His words, of course, were intended to inspire us to tap into our dreams for ourselves.

But I would ask a slightly different question: What are you willing to fight for, even if the odds are stacked against you, even if you'll most likely lose? In answering *that* question, you'll find what's really important to you. You'll define not just your dreams, but the essence of who you are.

In my life, I've found the things worth fighting for are always the hardest. And there is so much to be gained in fighting the fight, even when we fail. I suppose that is why I stubbornly resist the temptation to leave my home state of Texas, where movement toward progressive values can often feel like an unattainable goal. Even when, though I successfully filibustered for thirteen hours to stop a sweeping anti-abortion bill from passing, the governor called another session and passed it anyway. Even when the equal pay law that I had successfully fought to pass was vetoed. Even when I failed in my fight to better fund our public schools. There is meaning in each of those fights, in speaking truth and giving voice to unpopular causes.

And so, even as I found myself reeling from my gubernatorial campaign loss, I was still able to reflect on the treasured gifts I had taken away from the race. Young people from around the country came to work on the campaign, many of them telling me I'd helped them to connect with their passion for justice, and their desire to lift up the powerless, the unheard. People of all ages from very humble backgrounds volunteered at nights and on weekends, even though they were working full-time, because they believed so strongly in reshaping our state into one that provided a voice and opportunity for all.

Over 34,000 people volunteered their energy to making a difference. And a record number of people—over 180,000—contributed financially to the campaign, most of them in very low dollar amounts. It's the kind of donation that represents true sacrifice in a family budget already stretched too thin. We were a team, collectively fighting to create the better world we wanted.

A year later, I can clearly see the mark we made. We helped to create a whole new generation of activists in our state, so many of whom have kept right on swinging and fighting the progressive fight. They fucking hate to lose, too. There is so much power in that. And I look at their efforts with tremendous pride.

So, on days like November 3, 2015, when Houston's anti-discrimination "HERO" ordinance failed at the ballot box, and when the seduction of giving up begins to creep in, I think of all the people across the country who are out there giving it all they've got in the face of long odds. I marvel at the young people like Patrisse Cullors, Opal Tometi, and Alicia Garza behind the #blacklivesmatter movement, at young women like Emma Sulkowicz hefting her dorm-room mattress with her everywhere she went for over a year, sending a powerful message against campus sexual assault.

Closer to home, I marvel at young Sadie Hernandez from the Rio Grande Valley who staged a three-week protest in front of the Governor's Mansion because of cuts in cancer-screening funds to Planned Parenthood. I look with awe at the students at Mizzou who stood together against racial injustice and drove concrete change.

Such was my mind-set as I spoke to my campaign team that day after we lost. After lamenting how much I hate losing, I reminded them of all the lives they had touched, all the people they inspired. I reminded them of Teddy Roosevelt's rousing words: "It is hard to fail, but it is worse never to have tried to succeed." I asked my team to take pride in our daring to do something great, something hard. I asked them to own their courage and told them the only way we will have failed is if we give up and stop trying. And I asked them to keep up the fight, for themselves, for people they had met along the way, and for people they will never know.

Don't get me wrong. I still think that losing sucks. And it's okay to hate losing. That hatred provides us with the drive to face great challenges. But the losses I've endured have taught me that I am more powerful than the limitations of failed efforts. So my advice to you: If you fail, fail big! Fail with flair! Fail trying to do something real, something hard.

And when you do, own the journey with pride. Look at each battle scar you've earned as a tiny crack that will heal and make you stronger. And, as we'd say in Texas, get back up on that horse and ride to see another day.

GO YOUR OWN WAY

WE STARTED the JOURNEY

toward feminism

with the idea that some people choose to follow a map while others wander and take detours before falling into a path that leads them to the party. As we explored the means and ways, as well as the insights and aha moments, it became clear that feminism isn't one single thing. It's a whole host of ideas, of beliefs, of lifestyles, of passions. That variety is what makes it so great.

In this final section of essays and art, let's take a look at the ways people have made feminism an integral part of their lives. This section is a bit of everything: how one writer channeled his work as an EMT and activist into creating feminist art, a writer who decided to create her own reading syllabus dedicated to women's work after being told that no women had published anything worthwhile, and pieces that explore how, sometimes, we know who we are in high school—and we know who we aren't.

Go ahead. Go your own way with feminism. What you bring to the party and what inspires you are as important as the party itself.

Many Stories, Many Roads

BY DANIEL JOSÉ OLDER

> Caminante, son tus huellas el camino,
> y nada más; caminante,
> no hay camino, se hace camino al andar.
>
> Wanderer, your footsteps are the road,
> and nothing more; wanderer,
> there is no road, the road is made by walking.
>
> —ANTONIO MACHADO

I dreamed once that I was in a big, wide-open room with everyone I knew. The building was something like a renovated barn; sunlight poured in through large windows all around us. We were dancing. The dance was part coordinated, part spontaneous—a wild and free expression of all the love and sorrow we'd lived. Some moved in perfect time with one another, slowing down to make sure everyone knew the steps and then speeding up again; others moved in solos.

Imagine feminism is like that room—there have been so many journeys taken to arrive there. Who gets to show up and who gets to stay matters, as do the ways we each found the door and how we walked in.

Feminism, like so many other movements, has suffered from gatekeeping and line drawing—racism, homophobia, classism, and transphobia, among other oppressions, have acted like overzealous bouncers, keeping so many dancers out of that big beautiful room. And we forget sometimes, as we try to figure out when to fall into step and when to break away, how much our journeys, both individual and collective, matter.

It was January 2005. I was confused and brokenhearted and Latino and twenty-five, wandering the crooked cobblestone streets of Barcelona and trying to make sense of where I'd come from and where I was going. In high school, I wouldn't have called myself a feminist, but I had learned to listen to women, knew that there was some responsibility that came with being a man in this society that had nothing to do with chivalry or machismo. I knew the feeling of wanting to tear this unfair world up and build a more just one for the people I loved. I had been doing anti-racist organizing since college and worked as a paramedic in the streets of New York for the past few years, carrying the broken bodies of my brothers and sisters to area hospitals, and occasionally laying sheets over them and checking off the "Dead on Arrival" box on my paperwork. Dealing with violence against women firsthand became a part of the routine—an occurrence so common, it simply became a part of the crisis-laced backdrop of heart attacks, shootings, and overdoses. I took a step back. If men abusing women was part of a normal night for a first responder, what did that say about the larger world? Patterns of power and violence stood out starkly in the Brooklyn night, and I knew the answer for me would never be as straightforward as taking the same patients to the hospital again and again.

To maintain our privilege, we remain silent in the face of slowly unfolding disasters. We think if we don't mention it, it'll go away and we can keep pretending everything's okay. And our silence invites that tragedy in, entwines us even more inextricably. Of course, our silence won't protect us or anyone else, as Audre Lorde taught us; instead, it provides the dangerous illusion of safety. And so the cycle continues, unabated.

But the question of how to speak out, what it meant to protest, loomed large. In college, it had been pretty straightforward: identify a symptom and tie it to the underlying community norms, take over an event or a building, start a conversation. Out in the wider world, the geography of protest was complicated by nonprofits, grants, and a whole deeper labyrinth of politics and history that seemed to choke inspiration and spontaneity.

I had some semblance of a map in my mind, the beginnings of a language making sense of power and privilege, and no idea what to do with it or how to place myself within that messy intersection. That language, the one we use to understand this troubled world, is so personal—we each must cobble one together from what we've lived through and the wisdom of others. It's ever-evolving, ebbing and flowing, and at that moment, mine was still mostly gibberish.

But what did make sense to me was art. Specifically, the art of story. I knew how to feed the heartache of a shattered romance through the spinning gears of my imagination and transform it into a narrative arc. I'd spent the past few weeks conceiving a wild puppet show in an old spiral notebook—an impossible love amid dictatorship, an exile, music, and the tide of history—and I already knew that the act of creating this fictional truth from the ashes of a lived truth was my own way of crawling back to life.

So I came to Barcelona, where I walked, confused and heartbroken and Latino and twenty-five, down the crooked cobblestone streets until I came out at the throughway along the ocean and looked up to see the silhouette of Columbus glaring hungrily across the Atlantic. I thought about the terrible tides of history and all the slow tragedies that led to the world being the way it was, the violence of politics and resource wars and the battle lines drawn within my own family tree, the firing range that is identity itself for so many people of color. I thought about complicity, my own role as one who watched while the world spun past. I thought about a girl I had loved and lost, and another who'd loved me and lost me, and how language still couldn't encompass all the ways I felt about that ache. And in a very sudden and simple way, all those thoughts smashed together like a conflagration of tidal waves over the statue of that man the explorer who symbolized destruction to so many and somehow pride to so many others. And all the sorrows, huge and historical and minute and personal, became one. It sounds terrible, but the truth is, there was peace in that moment—a startling peace that took my breath away.

Inside me, a wall had collapsed. I turned my back on Columbus with his hungry glare and walked up into the Gothic City, toward the great cathedral that glared down from a hill over Barcelona. I thought about bell hooks, who so perfectly cuts through right to the political and emotional heart of the matter. Her essays had been an invitation into the great big room that is feminism, a call for inclusiveness, an anthem of nuance and bravery. I thought about James Baldwin, who alchemized rage and sorrow into literature, and Eduardo Galeano and Arundhati Roy. I carried their words with me like holy relics as I walked, along with the dead and injured I'd come across in the streets of New York and my own life, my own loved ones. They all walked with me, released by the newly shattered wall.

What was organizing if not telling a story? My path steepened up a hill; gardens rose on either side. A protest didn't have to fit a pattern; in fact, maybe it shouldn't ever. Maybe that was the problem. A part of my brain had awakened. I already had the language. The same tools I used to make art could go to work on the problem of protest. It was, after all, the same heart breaking, the same sense of joy at recovering the shattered pieces, at remembering we can love again. And we can love again, I realized as the city spread out before me. We can love again.

Patriarchy has sharp teeth. The borders it draws around our identities and hearts are unforgiving and lined with broken glass and barbed wire. Chimamanda Ngozi Adichie calls masculinity "a hard, small cage." Our patriarchal gender norms, the rules that tell us how to fit into pre-assigned boxes labeled "man" and "woman," have nothing to do with love and everything to do with power. They guide our steps and demolish our lives, our sense of self, our relationships. Because we have subscribed to them as a society, because they are normalized, they seep into our hearts and minds from our earliest contact with the world around us. They take root there, then metastasize.

My own journey to feminism required looking both outward and inward. It is an ongoing process that means learning and relearning how to listen, when to shut up, when to speak up. There is no map for the work of undoing that trauma within us—like all the great journeys, it is a road we make by walking. This is terrifying at first; there's a false comfort in the sense that if we just follow these simple steps, we will get where we need to go.

But the harder truth contains its own truer joy—the beautiful struggle. It requires us to enlist our creativity, our ability to love again, our courage, and perhaps most of all, our ability to simultaneously confront our own privilege and oppression, our own difficult histories as we come together, teaching one another brand-new steps in that great, sunlit hall.

THAT'S WHAT SHE BECAME by Jen Talley

she needed a hero

so that's what she became

Reading Worthy Women

BY NOVA REN SUMA

The dream captured me when I was twelve years old.

It climbed the mountain where we lived at the time, in an isolated rental on a dead-end dirt road, no TV reception, no Internet because it didn't exist yet, little connection to the outside world apart from the books on our shelves and those borrowed from the library in town. There was nowhere to go when my stepfather's moods turned, nowhere to hide but inside the pages of books. The dream found me there, the year I was the new kid at school, trying to survive the seventh grade during the day and my family's tense situation at night. It wedged its way inside me, and it grew.

The dream was to be a writer.

The dream was to publish books.

I didn't know any writers, not in real life—to me, they were mythical beings, like the gods walking the earth in my illustrated copy of *D'Aulaires' Book of Greek Myths*—so this dream felt crazy sometimes. It felt flimsy. In the beginning, anyone could have stolen it away from me with one harsh word.

Still, it grew.

Left to my own devices in the house after school, looking after my little sister and little brother while my mother and stepfather were at work, I ran out of books of my own and so had to raid the shelves in the living room. My stepfather had a sizable Stephen King and Dean Koontz collection, all of which I read, as well as some unsettling alien-abduction books (nonfiction? fiction? I wasn't sure) and some boring auto manuals I skipped over. It was my mother's bookshelves that called to me. There, I found the paperbacks she bought at garage sales and used bookstores, her crammed stacks of novels, so many, seeming more and more each week. These were books written by women. These were books *about* women, sometimes about girls. Like me.

I was twelve years old when I discovered Margaret Atwood on my mother's bookshelves. And Alice Walker. Marge Piercy. Louise Erdrich. And more.

I was twelve when I realized there could be real books about girls, and that stories about girls were important enough to be told.

I wrote about it in my diary. I decided I wanted to write stories like this, too. I told my mother, because back then I told her everything. But apart from her, I kept the dream mostly to myself. My dream involved writing, and it always felt connected to something else, something born I think of our life at home with my stepfather. Escape.

The dream—to grow up and be a writer—became my parachute. I would have fought anyone with my fists if they tried to grab it away.

"You can do anything you want to do."

That's what my mother said to me, when we were holed up in my room, avoiding my stepfather. I was her oldest, her first daughter, her most quiet and shyest child, and the one with the biggest, most unwieldy dreams.

There have been many people who have not believed in me over the years. My mother was not one of them. She fed me feminist literature and never saw me as insignificant, never too small. To acknowledge my first period, she bought me my first copy of *Our Bodies, Ourselves*, which taught me what it meant to be a girl and one day a woman in this world, and how I'd have to rely on myself for many things. My mother, who had let go of her dreams—to be an artist, a fashion designer—instilled some new dreams into me. She whispered in my ear, even when she herself felt trapped, that I could go anywhere, do anything, become whatever I hoped to be.

I would be a writer one day, like the women on my mother's bookshelves.

This is what I decided when I was twelve, before I realized that my dream, in some people's eyes, had boundaries. Limits. Before the men in my life showed me that my dream had a ceiling beyond which I could not and should not try to imagine myself reaching.

All because I was a girl.

We moved again, twice more, and there I was, still dreaming my escape. I was sixteen, maybe seventeen. Now we lived in a different patch of mountains, in a different rented house, in a different school district. Over the years, as my mother and stepfather switched jobs and found and lost opportunities, we kept moving, and the shell I had formed around myself grew thornier, harder to cut through. I was in there, somewhere, but if you met me among a group of people, you might never witness me peek out. My shyness made it hard for me to speak up, afraid to show who I really was. Sometimes it was easier to go along with things, pretend I was like everyone else. Sometimes the shell shifted, changed, depending on who I was hanging around with, who I wanted to impress.

But, at home, in my room with my door closed, I kept writing. On the page—in the poems I wrote back then, in the short stories—I was only myself. This was how I raised my voice, how I stopped hiding. It was the only way I knew how to speak.

I was sixteen, maybe seventeen. It was junior or senior year in my public high school in the Hudson Valley of New York State. Some of the details are smudged. The details that aren't glare back at me, brightly colored, difficult to shake. They show me how a small thing can turn singular and important. How one remark can set you on a course that will end up changing the rest of your life.

The class was World Humanities, and as I remember, it was a require-ment to get a Regents diploma, which was what I was aspiring to. World Humanities was a class in which we'd study literature, art, and music from around the world. It was taught by a teacher who was serious, passionate about his subject matter, and surely prided himself on the fact that his class was rumored to be fun. Some days we'd read plays aloud, performing differ-ent roles. Some days we'd spend the whole class listening to records with the fluorescent lights dimmed.

I was excited because I knew we'd be reading books. I'd be discovering new authors, ones beyond the scope of my parents' bookshelves or from my own explorations in the library.

I was paging through the syllabus, stirred at all the possibilities in the coming weeks, when it dawned on me.

I had to go back to check, to be sure.

Then I was sure: There were no women writers on the class syllabus. There wasn't one woman author, poet, or playwright.

There were no women artists on the syllabus. There wasn't one woman painter, sculptor, or photographer.

There weren't any female composers or musicians.

Out of every name listed on the syllabus—and this was a World Humanities class, meant to encompass arts from multiple disciplines across history, from all over the planet—there were no women.

The syllabus was all men.

I remember how this washed over me, and the conflicting emotions that came with it: confusion (was it an oversight, a mistake?), annoyance (maybe this class wouldn't be so fun after all), and then, quiet at first and then louder, the anger came.

I wanted to say something.

Yet, remember: I was shy. Still, even at that age, I had trouble speaking up in groups and turned, helplessly, an alarming shade of red when called on in class. I had never argued a thing, to any teacher. I wasn't the kind of student who would call out this problem with the syllabus in front of everyone, in the middle of class.

And yet, also remember: I was a girl who wanted to grow up to be a woman writer, and I was looking at a survey of the arts from all across the world in which not one woman was included.

I stayed behind after class to speak to the teacher. I remember the room, the large circle of desks, the record player against the wall, the window-panes that showed the track field in the distance, the football goal posts, and beyond that a glimpse of the rising mountains. I remember standing there for quite a while, fidgeting, uncomfortable in my shoes. My teacher was speaking to another student, a boy. This boy took all his attention, even though I was standing right there.

Finally, the boy left, and it was me and the teacher.

I wanted to ask something, I blurted out, probably faltering, fumbling, losing the words on my tongue.

Why, I asked my teacher, *why* were there no women on the syllabus?

I will tell you what he told me.

There were no women on the syllabus, my teacher said, because there were no women *worthy* of being on his syllabus.

No women who were worthy. These words sunk in.

Not one woman author, poet, or playwright. Not one woman painter, sculptor, or photographer. Not one woman composer or musician.

Not one female artist, at all, in the entire world was deemed worthy enough to be taught in the World Humanities class in our small-town high school.

What should I have said to that?

I know what I would say now, but I also can't help but acknowledge who I was then. The truth is, I don't think I said much. I can't now remember what words, if any, tumbled out of my mouth in response. I left the room.

Imagine what this story from my past could have been had I been a stronger, louder, more confident girl. If I'd said something smart back at him. If I'd laughed, maybe. If I'd called him out on being sexist. If I'd organized a protest in front of the whole school. If I'd dropped the class, even if it was a credit I needed to graduate. If I'd revealed myself to be the fearless feminist I was inside, past my shyness, down deep below my shell. If I'd done something other than walk out of the room.

Imagine that story. Then again, maybe it wouldn't have been such a story after all, because what happened wouldn't have changed me as much as it did.

Instead, it hit me, hard. It wormed into me. It would not, for the life of me, let go. I thought of all the women writers I'd read. Was he truly saying that nothing any woman had written was worthy of being read in this class?

I'd recently discovered Toni Morrison. I'd read *Beloved, Song of Solomon, Sula* . . . He didn't think that *Toni Morrison*, of all writers in all the world, was worthy?

Of course, I also turned the question on myself. I was no Toni Morrison (and who is?!), but still . . . Did this mean that in the outside world beyond my bedroom that nothing I'd ever write would be worthy, simply because I was a girl?

That I might as well stop now before I even started?

I refused to believe this.

I had to prove him wrong.

That was how my private, personal rebellion was born. It began from that brief conversation about one syllabus with one closed-minded teacher. Just like the dream that had taken me over years before—it got its hold on me, it settled, it grew.

My private rebellion was this: I decided I would read books written only by women.

Not including books that were assigned in my classes, but in my personal time, the books I *chose* to read—and I was a voracious reader—from then on would be only by women. Women of all backgrounds and nationalities. Women of all colors. Women of all sexual orientations and identities. But women. Only women. No men.

I would buy books written only by women. I would take out books from the library that were written only by women. The books I would share with friends, the books I would talk about, the books that filled my life, would be by women and only women, from then on.

This was my quiet pursuit, my way of being strong and making a statement, for myself.

The more I read like this, the more necessary it felt to keep going. So many of the books we'd been made to read throughout high school were written by men, old or dead white men, and so many of the stories were about men, about boys. It's well-known that girls are expected to connect to men's stories—these are the stories that are considered universal, the stories meant to speak to everyone. The classics. That's what was surrounding me. Men's stories. Men's lives. This man's world.

My World Humanities teacher was one thing. There was also what was happening at home.

There was my stepfather, the man who made our house unlivable, the reason I had my eyes on the door. When he heard I wanted to become a writer, he laughed and said, "Who would ever want to read anything you wrote?"

There was my father, a man who, upon hearing I wanted to go to college to study writing, turned to me and in all seriousness told me that my dreams were an illusion. Were effectively fluff. Instead, I should be practical. I should do something more suited to my mind. He randomly suggested I become a dental technician.

This had become personal. I wanted to prove my teacher wrong, yes. I wanted to prove my stepfather wrong and my father wrong.

But more than that, I wanted to prove it to *myself.*

My personal, private reading rebellion had one purpose only: I wanted to see—on my own—that women were just as worthy as men.

All told, my private reading rebellion lasted about five years. It carried me through the end of high school. It followed me through all four years of college (I did leave home, with my mother's support; I did escape with college scholarships and financial aid, as did she, with a divorce and a return to school to study art therapy not too many years later).

I read so many women over those years. I wish I'd kept track, because the list would be gorgeous and exciting and very, very long. I read more Toni Morrison. I read Edna St. Vincent Millay and Anne Sexton and Sylvia Plath and Audre Lorde and Sharon Olds and Nikki Giovanni. I read

Sandra Cisneros. Maxine Hong Kingston. Doris Lessing. Zora Neale Hurston. Isabelle Allende. Kathy Acker. Jeanette Winterson. Jamaica Kincaid. Jean Rhys. It wasn't until after college that I started reading men again.

This ended up shaping who I was as a young woman and led me to become the writer I am today. I learned from the women who came before me. I was influenced by them, inspired by them, fired up by them, led forward by them.

In the years I was reading for myself, I did find, and pretty quickly, that women were worthy. That was no surprise. What I also found was more personal. Through their words, I discovered my own words, my own voice.

Now, here I am. I've published four novels. I've found a way to overcome my shyness, and now I speak at conferences, at schools. I give readings from my books in front of crowds of people, exposing who I am through my words, the way the women authors I've admired did.

I've kept reading. Explore my bookshelves even today and you'll see that my taste tends to be stories written by women, stories about women and girls. In these books, I found a purpose. I found a light. I found a path to follow, a way. The question of worthiness has long been answered, my project closed down, but my love and hunger for these stories has only grown. Now my own books share these shelves.

I'm often asked why I write what I write: Why YA novels? Why books about teenagers? And beyond that, getting to the core of it: Why are my books always about *girls*?

My answer is connected to what I've said here: Because there are still people who don't think we're worthy, who think our stories are for our eyes only, who would not include our stories in a sweeping catalog of stories from around the world.

My extended period of reading only women took place in the 1990s, quite some time ago. Those five years illuminated my path as a female writer who writes stories exclusively, and without apology, about girls, knowing full well this may limit my audience. A writer who tells these stories with a fiery passion to prove they are just as important, and should be as universal, as stories about boys.

Those years easily proved my World Humanities teacher wrong, to the point where his syllabus didn't matter to me at all anymore. It had become about so much more.

You'd think that, by now, it would be obvious that women artists make incredible and worthy contributions to the world—just as incredible, just as worthy as men's contributions. You'd think that, by now, the work of women writers would be lauded the same as men's work, that there would be no discrepancy in the level of attention the media gives one over the other, that the women authors who effectively created what YA is today would be given their due. Yes, you would think so.

However, here we are in the field of YA and children's literature, still saying that women's work isn't treated the same as men's by the world at large. Here we are in the field of YA and children's literature, fighting for more diverse voices—under-represented voices from all spectrums—because they are sorely lacking on all fronts. Here we are saying, "We still have a ways to go."

My reading rebellion may have taken place a long time ago, but it still feels relevant. It's not a silly pursuit to read beyond what's handed to you, to seek out new voices and leap over the usual books everyone's already talking about and see what you can find on your own.

Making definitive choices about what we spend our time on as readers can make a statement, a difference. We can lift other writers up, give space and attention to more voices than the ones that already have all the space and the attention.

There is power in what we choose to consume as readers, and there is power in what we choose to amplify, celebrate, and share.

What kinds of worthy stories have we not been reading because they aren't the ones that are already so loud?

Who will we be reading next?

SIX GREAT COMICS BY WOMEN, ABOUT WOMEN, FOR EVERYONE

By Brenna Clarke Gray

1. *Captain Marvel* by Kelly Sue DeConnick

   This comic was a huge step forward for the community of women who love comics, because its exciting and empowering story lines gave women a place to rally. It was also actively marketed to women in a way comics often aren't—and it sold like gangbusters, proving that women love comics, too.

2. *Friends with Boys* by Faith Erin Hicks

   A homeschooled girl has to transition to life in a public school. Will her relationship with her brothers help or hinder her in everything that comes next? And will she learn to be friends with girls, too?

3. *Lumberjanes* by Grace Ellis and Noelle Stevenson

   This is a comic about the summer camp you always wished you could go to. If you love adventure and girl power, feminism and friendship, and women who transform into bears, this comic is for you.

4. *Ms. Marvel* by G. Willow Wilson

   This is the story of a young Muslim girl who, while trying to manage life trapped between her strict parents and the popular kids at school, finds herself with superpowers and tasked with the role of protecting Jersey City.

5. *This One Summer* by Mariko and Jillian Tamaki

   Everyone has that one summer that seems to change everything; this is the story of one such summer, as a girl comes to terms with her body, boys, and who her mother really is under all her sadness.

6. *Tomboy* by Liz Prince

   This is a personal memoir about not feeling like you fit in with the expectations people have for girls. What if you'd rather play with the boys—and what does that mean for the way the rest of the world treats you?

FAQs ABOUT FEMINISM

For people who have power in society, being questioned about that power or being forced to examine their biases or prejudices incites fear. Those with power are being challenged about why they've been given rights and privileges that not everyone has; no longer are they just permitted to accept those rights and privileges as being the way of the world, because such is definitely not the case. Feminism begs all people to think about the social, political, cultural, and economic power we have based on our sex, education, gender, and a whole host of other statuses we may or may not choose to have.

The Choice Is Yours

BY KODY KEPLINGER

I don't want to have kids.

That might seem like a weird topic, considering this book is for teenagers, but I'm guessing some of you feel the same way. But this essay isn't just about deciding whether or not to be a mother one day; it's about choices. Because, as girls, there are certain choices you are *expected* to make. And sometimes, when you don't want to follow the path that's expected, it's going to upset people. Even if it's not really any of their business.

Case in point: the future residential status of your womb.

I don't remember deciding not to have children. All I know is, even in elementary school, anytime I played with a baby doll, it was never my kid. It wasn't that I didn't like babies. I loved them. But I was always the babysitter, the big sister, maybe even the aunt, but never the mom. In fact, if I ever played house with my cousins and someone suggested I be the mom, I was likely to pack up my toys and announce, "I'm not playing, then."

Yeah, sometimes I was *kind of* a brat.

I couldn't have been older than eight or so the first time I told someone in my family that I didn't want to have babies when I grew up. And I still remember the response: "You'll change your mind."

I remember because I heard this exact phrase repeated over and over again. Whenever I told anyone my future plans, and that those plans lacked offspring, I'd be met with that same refrain, an assurance that I'd change my mind one day.

This only served, of course, to make me absolutely furious. Especially as I entered my high school years, at which point I thought, surely, people would take me seriously.

What I began to realize is that teenage girls' choices and opinions are often dismissed or ignored. Whether it's your favorite books or movies being referred to as "girl stuff," and therefore less than. Or someone calling you "emotional" or "dramatic" rather than hearing you out about your feelings. Or, the absolute worst, adults telling you it's "just a phase" whenever you do something they don't understand.

And, okay, maybe sometimes it *is* just a phase, but adults go through phases frequently and no one makes them feel like crap about it.

Besides, I'm in my mid-twenties and I still sport pink hair every so often, so just a phase? I think not.

And in this case, the "norm" is—or is presumed to be—wanting children. The assumption is that all women eventually want babies. That it's just part of our DNA, and one day our biological clocks go crazy and we all have baby fever.

This has always bothered me. For one, because it implies that women are nothing more than wombs with legs. But, for another, it suggests that we can't make choices about those wombs. That we are ruled by our hormones and that, because of this, we lack the ability to make decisions about our own lives.

"But . . . why don't you want kids?"

On the rare occasions I was able to get someone to take me seriously enough to go beyond the assertions that I'd change my mind, I'd get this question. Because wanting kids is seen as "normal," not wanting them is "abnormal," and therefore, a solid reason is required.

"Do you hate kids?"

"Nope. I love kids."

"Are you just scared of getting fat?"

"What? No!"

"Is it because you don't want to pass on your disability?"

This one always takes me by surprise, no matter how many times I hear it.

I'm legally blind because of a somewhat rare genetic condition. One that, there is a slim chance, could be passed on. Though, honestly, I'd never really even thought of that as a problem. Definitely not something that would keep me from having kids if I wanted them.

And it hurts that anyone would even assume this was my reason, because it implies that I'd rather just not have babies to avoid the remote possibility of bringing another legally blind child into the world. It suggests that, maybe, I've wished I was never born. And that's so far from the truth that it's mind-blowing.

Because I've been asked so often, I have crafted a list of reasons I don't want kids. Here are the top three, in reverse order.

3.) I don't even know how to put a diaper on a kid, and I have no interest in learning.

2.) The idea of pushing a human being out of my body is less than appealing to me.

1.) Really, I just don't want them.

My disability is nowhere on this list. And if, someday, a miracle happens and I *do* change my mind, it won't be a factor then, either.

"But, Kody, not wanting kids is just selfish."

This idea has always confused me, but it seems to be a common one. It's this notion that women who decide not to have children must be spending all of that extra time and money on themselves—on vacations or shopping. On self-indulgence rather than caring for a family.

Which . . . I don't really see how that's a bad thing?

Growing up, I was always warned against selfishness. I'm sure you were, too, and for the most part, I understand why. It's important to consider the feelings and livelihood of others. But I think, sometimes, girls aren't encouraged enough to think about themselves. It's why we apologize too often and why we blame ourselves for things we shouldn't.

And it's why we cringe at the notion of spending our time and money on ourselves rather than on children who don't even exist yet.

Think about that. Women who don't want children are seen as selfish because they'd rather spend their money and time on themselves rather than on *children who don't even exist yet*. That's not even the primary reason many women opt out of having kids, but if it were, why would that be a problem? Wouldn't it be more selfish to have kids if you know you'd rather spend the money on yourself?

I don't feel like guys get called "selfish" for making these decisions.

In the past few decades, there has been a significant rise in women choosing not to have kids. According to the U.S. Census Bureau's Current Population Survey, in 2014, nearly half of women between the ages of fifteen and forty-four were childless. That's the highest the number has ever been since the United States began recording these surveys. And one reason for this is that many women now choose to focus on their careers—a choice that is also frequently seen as selfish.

But here's the thing: we've worked for a long time for the ability to be selfish. This wasn't a choice women have always had. We've worked hard—and are still working hard—to create opportunities for women, to help women have choices when it comes to their futures. These choices did not always exist, and now that they do, many women have decided to chase those dreams, to put career ambitions at top priority, and for some, that includes choosing to remain childless.

And if that's something that you think you might want, I'm here to tell you—that's not selfish at all. We have choices for a reason, and while you might be encouraged or expected to take a certain path in your life, at the end of the day, it's your choice to make.

Maybe you already know you want children one day. Maybe you already know that you don't. And maybe you're in high school and have no clue what you want yet.

And maybe you'll change your mind.

That—all of that—is totally okay.

A Guide to Being a Teenage Superheroine

TEXT AND ILLUSTRATIONS BY
ALLISON PEYTON STEGER AND REBECCA SEXTON

So you want to be a superhero? Great! Making that decision is the first step, but there are a few other things you'll need to figure out before you hit the streets and start saving the day. Don't worry, our handy dandy guide will walk you through the process.

Before you know it, you'll be kicking ass and taking names, all in the cause of truth, justice, or whatever else you stand for.

STEP 1: HI, MY NAME IS . . .

Figuring out who you are and what you stand for is a lifelong process, but before anyone else gets to know you, it's best to at least know who you are *right now*. Besides, if you don't come up with your own superhero name, the 24-hour news cycle will and you'll miss out on an opportunity to bust out that awesome nickname you were saving for when you became a pop star or joined a worldclass dance crew (not that becoming a superhero will preempt you from achieving those goals!). While you're at it, go ahead and give yourself an origin story. Origin stories are full of heartbreak and misery, so whatever shit you survived: it's turning you into the superheroine you're becoming.

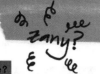

zany?

What will your name be?

"Amazing" and "Incredible" are played out adjectives. Get yourself a thesaurus. Try:

- Startling
- Inconceivable
- Churlish
- Thaumaturgic [means miraculous!]
- Spooky
- Delightful

When giving yourself a title, be bold! "Captain" is used up. Try:

- Admiral
- Baroness
- Mother Superior
- Chancellor
- Dame
- The Right Honorable
- Sultaness

Also consider occupations or hobbies!

- The [Adjective] Carpenter!
- [Title] Seamstress!   *Seamstress*
- [Your name], Esquire
- The Knitting [Noun with a K]
- The Tweeting Titan

If you're going to be The [Blank] [Gender], consider avoiding "Girl" and going with "Woman," "Lady," or "Gal," (if that's your gender identity) as these will age better if you plan to continue your superhero career into adulthood.

Alliteration: Fun, but not necessary.

Don't discount puns--it works for Roller Derby Girls. Talk about superheroines!

- Can't-Miss Everdeen
- Bella Strong
- Alice in Thunderland
- Leslie Nope

What will your powers be?

Are your powers magnifications of stuff you can already do?

- Your eyerolls can convince people to reconsider their poor decisions!
- Your matchmaking skills can bring about world peace!
- Your school spirit inspires people to band together and work toward a common goal!
- Your research skills expose the failings of the rich and powerful! (Traditionally, research is the sidekick's job, but there's no reason to be hemmed in by expectations here.)

Technology based, physical strength based, or magic based? (Why not try all three!)

Are your powers ready to go at all times, or are they activated by some sort of object/emotion/event/person? (i.e, you need your Magical Crystal of Righteous Indignation to get going, or maybe we won't like you when you're angry.)

What is your cause?

- Do litterbugs make you see red?
- Are you ready to dismantle the patriarchy?
- Do you want to take down the 1%?
- Do you want to stand up to the substitute teacher who deliberately mispronounces your name?
- Are you dedicated to taking down online trolls?
- Or real trolls?
- Do you want to keep your superheroing a secret or go public with your dual identities?

STEP 2: DOES THIS OUTFIT MAKE ME LOOK SUPER?

Superheroes wear costumes. It's pretty much a given. By now you already know the power of a good outfit to help you feel confident and superhero-ing is no different! But there are some unique variables to take into account.

- **MOST IMPORTANT RULE:** Form follows function!

- **FOUNDATIONAL GARMENTS:** if you usually wear a bra, you'll want to step your game up here. A good sports bra is your truest friend in the fight against injustice.

- **RUNNING SHOES VS. HIKING BOOTS:** do you want to go fast or go hard? (Heels only if your superpower involves only intellectual prowess and you will never have to get anywhere quickly.)

- **COLOR SCHEME:** traditionally, primary colors = good guys and secondary colors = bad guys, but don't let that hold you back. Plus, metallics and leopard print aren't even IN that breakdown. You do you.

- **PONYTAILS:** pretty much essential if you have long hair. French braids are pretty durable too, but harder to do on the fly.

- **DO YOU WEAR GLASSES?** Make sure they will stay on through all activity. (You can wear contacts, of course, but no need to limit glasses to your Clark Kent life if you don't want to.) If you think you're going to fight a lot of crime outdoors during the day, get cool sunglasses. And sunscreen. Nothing heroic about skin cancer, friends.

- **PANTS VS. DRESSES VS. BIKINIS:** pants have the most obvious functionality, but it all depends on your identity and comfort level. Just remember: how much skin you show is your own damn business, and what you do or don't reveal has no effect on how powerful you are.

- **WEAPONRY:** again, form follows function. Make sure you can quick draw whatever you've got.

- **YOUR LOGO:** very literal, super abstract, what do you want? Lots of room to try things out here. Think about placement, too.

- **AND DON'T FORGET SIZE AND CLARITY:** you don't want to end up in a Superman situation, with everyone thinking your family symbol is an "s" for "super."

- **HIDING YOUR IDENTITY:** domino masks are traditional, but you can wear a full-face mask and/or crazy makeup, too!

Feel free to try a bunch of different looks before committing to one. Everyone loves a makeover montage! And don't worry about being timeless. You can always do a redesign.

STEP 3 TO THE BATMOBILE!

Look, the bad guys are not gonna come to you, for the most part. You're gonna have to go to them. And to do that, you're gonna need some wheels. What sort of vehicle those wheels are attached to, though, is up to you.

What's your service area?

- Are you a hometown girl? Think local.
- Are you super patriotic? National might be the right fit for you.
- Are you a globetrotter? International superheroing will let you see the world.
- Are you out of this world? Intergalactic is also an option, but be warned: the logistics for this might be a nightmare!

Do you have a driver's license?

- If you do, great! That gives you some freedom and control.
- If you don't, no worries!

Batman has a pretty sweet car, and the Avengers have the Quinjet, and that's great, but look, public transportation and bicycles have their place too.

- Downside to having a fancy car to match your #brand: lack of anonymity. Depending on your whole look and approach, something a little more subtle might be a real asset. Plus, the MPG on the Batmobile must be just terrible, you'd have to be a billionaire to afford it.

- Not to mention, insurance! If you have your own vehicle, it's important to have coverage. Realistically, you are going to get into more accidents than a non-superhero, including occasional harm to bystander property, and a superheroine always pays her deductible so her insurance can make up the rest.

Consider something self-propelled to avoid traffic jams or the vagaries of public transportation schedules.

- Jet boots could be fun!
- Skateboard: get where you're going and have fun and look cool doing it.
- Technically, Segways meet this qualifier and already exist, but don't jet boots seem cooler?
- Real talk: a bicycle is self-propelled, fits a lot of places a car won't, and think how great your weapon will look sticking out of your wicker basket.

STEP 4: WHO YOU GONNA CALL?

Listen, it's true what they say: it takes a village. No matter what or who you're fighting, you don't have to do it alone. And while it's okay to work solo—superhero teams can be a little like dysfunctional families—it still helps to have someone who can cover for you with your mom, fix your broken gadgets, mend your torn costumes, and have hot chocolate with you after a long day on the job.

Are you a solo operative, part of a team or organization, or sometimes one, sometimes another?

- If you are part of an organization or a team, remember: your guiding light has to be your own ethical judgment and sense of right and wrong. If you've gotta flip a table and storm out at some point, well, you're in fine superhero company.

If you decide to go with a secret identity, who do you trust with that secret?

- You may decide you don't want to tell anybody because, it's true, anyone who knows your secret will be in a little danger themselves. But, your loved ones will probably think the risk is worth it to support you. Besides, you might be in a little less danger yourself if you've got backup you can count on. And honestly, do you really think you can keep something this cool to yourself?

Sidekicks:

- Calling a friend or classmate your sidekick might make her feel undervalued or unappreciated. If you want to work closely with another person, considering making her your partner.

- For an actual sidekick, consider an unusual pet with a useful skill set. A velociraptor is a great intimidation tool. A unicorn can help you solve your transportation problems.

- Little brothers could be okay in this role, too.

- Whoever you pick, remember: no one is the sidekick in their own life. Respect that they have other things going on, even if they're a dinosaur (or a little brother).

Even solo heroes need a great behind-the-scenes team. Here are some people you may want to recruit to help you out, and definitely let these people know how much you value them. Holidays off and cake on every birthday:

- THE RESEARCHER. Do you have a friend whose nose is always stuck in Wikipedia? Who never leaves home without her library card? That's your information seeker. They say to "know thy enemy." She's invaluable on that front.

- THE COSTUME DESIGNER. This is your friend who always has the right outfit for any occasion, keeps a change of clothes in her car, and knows how to sew on a button. Ask her to help you keep your costume looking and feeling good. If she says no capes, let her have that one.

- THE TECH WIZARD. You'll need, at the very least, a reliable communications system and GPS for effective superheroing. Do you have a friend who once got grounded for dismantling the toaster oven? That's your gadget guru.

- THE NURSE'S AIDE. Superheroing ain't easy. You're bound to get a few bumps and scrapes and you'll need a friend who doesn't faint at the sight of blood to bandage you up. Find a friend who wants to go to med school and gets excited for dissection day in Biology.

- THE FRENEMY. Okay, frenemy is kind of a strong word. But it's good to have someone around who challenges you or makes you look at a problem from another angle. Did someone beat you out for captain of the debate team? Consider adding her to your superhero team. Having someone smart, driven, and competitive around will push you to be your best.

- THE GROWN-UP. Buffy has Giles, Veronica has Keith, and Peter Parker has Aunt May. There are just some situations where adult help is necessary, so go ahead and have one on speed dial.

So there it is, our simple four-step process for saving the world and looking good doing it. But remember: there are as many ways to be a superheroine as there are badass women doing the superheroing. There's no one right way to make things better, help people, or make a difference. You get to decide for yourself what matters most to you, and how you personally are best equipped to tackle it. Follow your heart, trust your gut, and you'll be great.

And when we need you, we'll flip on the Batsignal. We feel better already, knowing you're out there.

Don't Peak in High School

MINDY KALING

Sometimes teenage girls ask me for advice about what they should be doing if they want a career like mine one day. There are basically three ways to get where I am: (1) learn a provocative dance and put it on YouTube; (2) persuade your parents to move to Orlando and homeschool you until you get cast on a kids' show; or do what I did, which is (3) stay in school and be a respectful and hardworking wallflower and go to an accredited non-online university.

Teenage girls, please don't worry about being super popular in high school or being the best actress or the best athlete. Not only do people not care about any of that the second you graduate, but when you get older, if you reference your successes in high school too much, it makes you look kind of pitiful, like some babbling Tennessee Williams character with nothing going on in her current life. What I've noticed is that almost no one who was a big star in high school is a big star later in life. For us overlooked kids, it's so wonderfully *fair*.

I was never the lead in the play. I don't think I went to a single party with alcohol at it. No one offered me pot. It wasn't until I was sixteen that I even knew marijuana and pot were the same thing. I didn't even learn this from a cool friend; I gleaned it from a syndicated episode of *21 Jump Street*. My parents didn't let me do social things on weeknights, because week-nights were for homework, and *maybe* an episode of *The X-Files* if I was being good (*The X-Files* was on Friday night), and *on extremely rare occasions*, I could watch *Seinfeld* (Thursday, a school night), if I had aced my PSATs or something.

It is easy to freak out as a sensitive teenager. I always felt I was missing out because of how the high school experience was dramatized in TV and song. For every realistic *My So-Called Life*, there were ten *Party of Five*s or *90210*s, where a twenty-something Luke Perry was supposed to be just a typical guy at your high school. If Luke Perry had gone to my high school, everybody would have thought, *What's the deal with this brooding greaser? Is he a narc?* But that's who Hollywood put forth as "just a dude at your high school."

In the genre of "making you feel like you're not having an awesome American high school experience," the worst offender is actually a song, John Cougar Mellencamp's "Jack & Diane." It's one of those songs—like Eric Clapton's "Tears in Heaven"—that everyone knows all the words to without ever having chosen to learn them. I've seen people get incredibly pumped when this song comes on; I once witnessed a couple request it four times in a row at Johnny Rockets and belt it while loudly clapping their hands above their heads, so apparently it is an anthem of some people's youth. I think across America, as I type this, there are high school couples who strive to be like Jack and Diane from that song. Just hangin' out after school, makin' out at the Tastee Freez, sneakin' beers into their cars, without a care in the world. Just two popular, idle, all-American white kids, having a blast.

The world created in "Jack & Diane" is maybe okay-charming because, like, all right, that kid Jack is going to get shipped off to Vietnam and there was going to be a whole part two of the story when he returned as some traumatized, disillusioned vet. The song is only interesting to me as the dreamy first act to a much more interesting *Born on the Fourth of July*-type story.

As it is, I find "Jack & Diane" a little disgusting.

A child of immigrant professionals, I can't help but notice the wasteful frivolity of it all. Why are these kids not home doing their homework? Why aren't they setting the table for dinner or helping out around the house? Who allows kids to hang out in parking lots? Isn't that loitering?

I wish there were a song called "Nguyen & Ari," a little ditty about a hardworking Vietnamese girl who helps her parents with the franchised Holiday Inn they run, and does homework in the lobby, and Ari, a hardworking Jewish boy who does volunteer work at his grandma's old-age home, and they meet after school at Princeton Review. They help each other study for the SATs and different AP courses, and then, after months of studying, and mountains of flashcards, they kiss chastely upon hearing the news that they both got into their top college choices. This is a song teens need to inadvertently memorize. Now that's a song I'd request at Johnny Rockets!

In high school, I had fun in my academic clubs, watching movies with my friends, learning Latin, having long, protracted, unrequited crushes on older guys who didn't know me, and, yes, hanging out with my family. I liked hanging out with my family! Later, when you're grown up, you realize you never get to hang out with your family. You pretty much only have eighteen years to spend with them full-time, and that's it. So, yeah, it all added up to a happy, memorable time. Even though I was never a star.

Because I was largely overlooked at school, I watched everyone like an observant weirdo, not unlike Eugene Levy's character Dr. Allan Pearl in *Waiting for Guffman*, who "sat next to the class clown, and studied him." But I did that with everyone. It helped me so much as a writer; you have no idea.

I just want ambitious teenagers to know it is totally fine to be quiet, observant kids. Besides being a delight to your parents, you will find you have plenty of time later to catch up. So many people I work with—famous actors, accomplished writers—were overlooked in high school. Be like Allan Pearl. Sit next to the class clown and study him. Then grow up, take everything you learned, and get paid to be a real-life clown, unlike whatever unexciting thing the actual high school class clown is doing right now.

The chorus of "Jack & Diane" is: "Oh yeah, life goes on, long after the thrill of livin' is gone."

Are you kidding me? The thrill of living was high school? Come on, Mr. Cougar Mellencamp. Get a life.

THIS PIECE WAS PREVIOUSLY PUBLISHED IN *IS EVERYONE HANGING OUT WITHOUT ME?* *(AND OTHER CONCERNS)* BY MINDY KALING.

Owning My Feminism

BY KELLY JENSEN

I took note of the girls who spoke out about feminism in college. They'd raise their hands proudly in class, share their experiences, and become impassioned to the point of tears about how women and people of color deserve better. They staffed student tables in the commons for feminist organizations and ran programs educating anyone who'd listen about the need for equality.

I watched as a fellow writer shared her work at open mics, in the classroom, and privately, with me, seeking my feedback. I always felt intimidated by her. Her words, her imagery, described worlds where girls were powerful, had a voice, and persevered through the heaviest stuff imaginable. She wrote what I wanted to say but couldn't.

One of my best friends volunteered at the local women's health clinic, counseling pregnant girls about their options. She asked me to join her many times, but I had too much homework. I was too tired. I needed to put in more hours at my job.

In truth, I was too scared.

In no way was I a capital-*F* Feminist like the incredible, dedicated women who surrounded me. I shied away from big discussions, from putting myself out there in a public way, from proudly and loudly owning the things I cared about deeply. My opinions didn't matter, because other people said it so much better. I needed time and space to polish my thoughts before I could raise my hand and speak.

Fear kept me back and told me I wasn't good enough to be one of those bold women pushing ahead and speaking up.

I was messy, unsure, ineloquent.

I felt like an impostor.

Still, I was drawn to writing about issues that affected girls and women. It was a talent I nurtured, but in private. It served as an activity for me and only me that let me work through the things I was thinking about in the way I best knew how. I wrote poetry about girls who weren't "feminine" or "proper" and had relationships with boys; the poetry wasn't easy to read because the girls took charge or observed things that would make an average reader uncomfortable. I wrote about girls who had intimate relationships with other girls. Girls who shared secrets and cigarettes with one another; girls who knew they were always being scrutinized and watched and judged by the world around them, for better or for worse.

The classes I took and papers I wrote in college frequently explored topics as they related to girls and women. My senior psychology thesis focused on how girls struggle more frequently than boys to settle in when they first go to college. Rates of mental health challenges and feelings of isolation and inadequacy are more likely to become worse in girls' first years away from home. One of the many reasons behind this is that girls thrive on the kinds of close relationships with other people that require time and energy to build.

It was in this paper, in my final hours of school, where all of the experiences through my four years of college made sense. My feminism wasn't just in performance. It wasn't on the front lines.

My feminism was in connections. In being there for others, a steady and solid rock, supporting, encouraging, and listening to the stories of those around me. Championing and challenging them.

And this was when it clicked: I *wasn't* an impostor. My feminism, though not the capital-F, out-loud style I saw around me, but more the quiet, internal, and intentionally *lowercase-f* feminism, was also valid.

Impostor Syndrome—the belief that your way isn't right, that your way doesn't matter, or that you're never going to know or be "enough" of something—is a real experience, and it's pernicious. It's also one of the reasons feminism, both the upper- and lowercase-*f* varieties, is important.

Society, culture, and the media constantly tell us we're not good enough and that our accomplishments and achievements don't matter or make a difference. But these are lies. Whatever it is that sets our hearts ablaze and whatever means we choose to pursue change in the world matter.

Every revolution starts with a spark, and every person finds that spark in their own way.

> The import is not the kind of work a woman does, but rather the quality of the work she furnishes. —EMMA GOLDMAN.

Emma Goldman, a feminist revolutionary and namesake of the women's clinic near my college, said the words that resonated with me both in college and now, many years later. The tools at my disposal for feminism were the very things that made me feel like a Feminist Impostor. I'd never be the girl hopping into a van to protest the closing of abortion clinics across the country, and I'd never be the girl who raised her hand high and proud in a classroom discussion to call out misogyny or slut shaming or racist or ableist language.

But I was the girl who could say it on paper and really listen to those who sought me out to talk through the big and small pieces of their lives, who needed a bit of encouragement to make their voices sharper and more assured.

I encouraged friends in their pursuits, holding space for them when their experiences and lives required it. I supported them, loved them, and reminded them that even when things got too hard to handle, it was okay to step back and take a break. To reassess. To try again.

I offered my critical eye and my time to those who wanted feedback on their creative work. I pushed them in private, suggesting they sharpen this line or read a passage out loud again and again until they saw where the meter broke or where the image just didn't fit. To kill their darlings so that the structure they were building, the words *they* were using, would shine bright.

My feminism was, and still is, lowercase. My strengths, listening and thinking, assessing and supporting, matter just as much as the strengths of louder, more visible feminists. My feminism makes a difference, too.

Maybe you can't name the women who led the suffragist movement, and maybe you can't list key dates in feminist history, or you weren't aware there were different waves of feminism. Those facts aren't the whole of feminism. Knowing them, or not, doesn't make your feminism more or less important.

Impostor syndrome is a nasty tool in the cultural arsenal of Keeping Power. Whatever drives you matters. It's not too much. It's not too little. Every step, the loud ones and the quiet ones, creates impact. My voice and your voice carry weight. We bring our own unique magic to the world, as long as we *use* those voices.

Own that magic and sprinkle it with passion. It matters because you matter.

You are not, nor will you ever be, an impostor.

INTERSECTIONAL ROSIE THE RIVETER
by Tyler Feder

ACKNOWLEDGMENTS

This book wouldn't have been possible without my editors, **Elise Howard** and **Krestyna Lypen**. Thank you to both of you for not only reaching out to me when I tweeted the idea but also for being excited by it and wanting to make my dream a reality. Thank you to **Sarah Alpert** for offering ideas and fielding questions, and thanks also to **Eileen Lawrence** and everyone else at **Algonquin**, especially in contracts, for making this happen. A big thank-you to my agent, **Tina Wexler**, for hopping into this project (and more!) midstream.

A few other individuals deserve some recognition for being brilliant, insightful, and all-around stand-up folks to have in my corner throughout the process of creating this anthology. These individuals have given me a little of everything—from eyes to ears to hearts and sometimes all three at once: **Andrea Vogt, Brandy Colbert, Courtney Summers, Justina Ireland, Katherine Sullivan, Kimberly Francisco, Leila Roy, Liz Burns, Trish Doller,** and **Sarah McCarry**. I consider myself immensely lucky to not only call you friends, but to know that you're always going to challenge me to dig a little deeper, push a little farther, and grow a little more.

To the ladies of Team Harpy: Not only did I get to create a dream anthology that talks about why feminism matters, but it's been great to bond with women like you who believe in the importance of putting your words into action.

I'd also like to thank **Jessica Spotswood** and **Amber J. Keyser** for helping me wrap my head around putting together an anthology early on. Your advice and insight were tremendous.

Thank you to the **brilliant contributors to this collection.** I cannot tell you how much I learned from each and every one of you. You made this work a joy, and I'm honored to have had the opportunity to work with you.

Mom and Grandma: Thanks for always letting me do what I wanted to do, read what I wanted to read, and handle things how I thought they were best handled. I'm so glad you didn't keep tabs on the library fines I racked up before I turned eighteen, because otherwise I'd be paying you back for eternity.

And always, thanks to **Erik.** We make a great team.

Further
READING

Throughout this anthology, you've found great lists of feminist art and media to consume. Likewise, many of the contributors to this collection are themselves authors who create feminist work. But maybe you're looking for even more. Once you start, you'll find it difficult to stop seeking out the kind of work that shares your values, that cherishes and respects you as a reader, and that begs you to take away something powerful and apply it into your life. Below you'll find excellent feminist fiction and nonfiction, as well as a wide selection of feminist films and websites that are more than worth your time. There's a little bit of everything here from memoirs to historical profiles to fantasy stories and more. Works by contributors aren't included—their works are cited in their respective bios.

FEMINIST FICTION

- *After the Fall* by Kate Hart
- *Alanna: The First Adventure (Song of the Lioness series)* by Tamora Pierce
- *Audacity* by Melanie Crowder
- *Beauty Queens* by Libba Bray
- *Bone Gap* by Laura Ruby
- *Bumped and Thumped* by Megan McCafferty
- *Castle Waiting* by Linda Medley
- *Code Name Verity* by Elizabeth Wein
- *The Disreputable History of Frankie Landau Banks* by E. Lockhart
- *Dreamland* by Sarah Dessen
- *Gabi, a Girl in Pieces* by Isabel Quintero
- *The Handmaid's Tale* by Margaret Atwood
- *Infandous* by Elana K. Arnold
- *A Mad, Wicked Folly* by Sharon Biggs Waller
- *Only Ever Yours* by Louise O'Neill
- *Otherbound* by Corinne Duyvis
- *Over You* by Amy Reed
- *Poisoned Apples: Poems for You, My Pretty* by Christine Heppermann
- *September Girls* by Bennett Madison

- *Speak* by Laurie Halse Anderson
- *Summer of Chasing Mermaids* by Sarah Ockler
- *The Summer Prince* by Alaya Dawn Johnson
- *Tithe (Modern Faerie Tales series)* by Holly Black
- *A Time to Dance* by Padma Venkatraman
- *A Tyranny of Petticoats* edited by Jessica Spotswood
- *Under a Painted Sky* by Stacey Lee
- *Where the Stars Still Shine* by Trish Doller

FEMINIST NONFICTION

- *Asking for It: The Alarming Rise of Rape Culture—and What We Can Do about It* by Kate Harding
- *Bossypants* by Tina Fey
- *The Butterfly Mosque* by G. Willow Wilson
- *Citizen* by Claudia Rankine
- *Claudette Colvin: Twice Toward Justice* by Phillip Hoose
- *Colonize This!: Young Women of Color on Today's Feminism* edited by Daisy Hernandez
- *Full Frontal Feminism* by Jessica Valenti

- *Headstrong: 52 Women Who Changed Science—and the World* by Rachel Swaby
- *Honor Girl* by Maggie Thrash
- *Hunger Makes Me a Modern Girl: a Memoir* by Carrie Brownstein
- *I Am Malala: The Girl Who Stood Up for Education and Was Shot by the Taliban* by Malala Yousafzai
- *A Little F'ed Up* by Julie Zeilinger
- *Persepolis* by Marjane Sartrapi
- *Rad American Women A–Z: Rebels, Trailblazers, and Visionaries Who Shaped Our History . . . and Our Future!* by Kate Schatz and Miriam Klein Stahl
- *Redefining Realness: My Path to Womanhood, Identity, Love, and So Much More* by Janet Mock
- *Rookie Yearbooks* edited by Tavi Gevinson
- *The Smart Girl's Guide to Privacy* by Violet Blue
- *Speak Up: A Guide to Having Your Say and Speaking Your Mind* by Halley Bondy
- *Stonewall: Breaking Out in the Fight for Gay Rights* by Ann Bausum
- *The V-Word* edited by Amber J. Keyser
- *We Should All Be Feminists* by Chimamanda Ngozi Adichi
- *Well-Behaved Women Seldom Make History* by Laurel Thatcher Ulrich
- *Women Heroes of the American Revolution: 20 Stories of Espionage, Sabotage, Defiance, and Rescue* by Susan M. Casey

FEMINIST FILMS

- *Alien*
- *Belle*
- *Bend It Like Beckham*
- *Bring It On*
- *. . . But I'm a Cheerleader*
- *Clueless*
- *The Craft*
- *Dark Girls*
- *Dirty Dancing*
- *Easy A*
- *Election*
- *Ginger Snaps*
- *A Girl Walks Home Alone at Night*
- *Girlhood*
- *Girls Rock!*
- *Jennifer's Body*
- *Killing Us Softly*
- *Legally Blonde*
- *The Magdalene Sisters*
- *Maleficent*
- *The Mask You Live In*
- *Miss Representation*
- *Now and Then*
- *Persepolis*
- *Precious*
- *Rabbit-Proof Fence*
- *Raise the Red Lantern*
- *Real Women Have Curves*
- *Sisterhood of the Traveling Pants*
- *Spirited Away*
- *We Are the Best*
- *Whale Rider*

WEBSITES BY AND ABOUT FEMINISTS/FEMINISM

- Autostraddle: autostraddle.com
- Badass Ladies You Should Know: badassladiesyoushouldknow.com
- Bitch Media: bitchmedia.org/articles
- Black Girl Nerds: blackgirlnerds.com
- Everyday Feminism: everydayfeminism.com
- The F-Bomb: thefbomb.org
- Feminist Frequency: feministfrequency.com
- Feministing: feministing.com
- Herself: herself.com
- Racialicious: racialicious.com
- Scarleteen: scarleteen.com
- Shakesville: shakesville.com

CONTRIBUTOR BIOS

Zariya Allen is an actress, writer, singer, and songwriter from Los Angeles. She is very excited to be a part of this project and to influence girls everywhere. She hopes to continue to use her art to not only entertain, but to effect change in the real world. If you'd like to follow up with her, visit zariyaallen.com or follow her on Instagram: @zariyaallen.

Stasia Burrington (nee Kato) was born in Texas, grew up in Montana, and now lives and works in Seattle with her favorite man and two cats. She is a full-time artist/illustrator. Her passions lie in the arts—in all forms—experimental cooking, camping, theology and science fiction, fat nerdy science books, coffee, and ice cream. She has illustrated books both for adults and for children, painted on buildings, helmets, and clothing, and strives to bring about just a little more compassion and beauty.

Brandy Colbert is the author of the critically acclaimed *Pointe*, and two forthcoming young adult novels. She lives and writes in Los Angeles. Visit her online at brandy colbert.com.

Wendy Davis is a former Democratic state senator from Texas known for her thirteen-hour filibuster to stop a sweeping anti-abortion bill's passage. In 2014, she lost her bid to become Texas's first Democratic governor since Ann Richards's election in 1990. But she's still swinging . . .

Mia DePrince was born in Sierra Leone, where she was abandoned as a two-year-old at the height of the civil war. When she was nearly five, she was adopted by an American family and fell in love with their piano. She now plays six instruments, composes music, and is an emerging singer/songwriter, majoring in songwriting. Mia, an advocate for civil liberties and the rights of women, is currently writing a book about her experiences as a child victim of war.

Orphaned by the civil war in Sierra Leone, **Michaela DePrince** found hope in a photograph of a ballerina, which she spotted on the cover of a magazine. After an American family adopted her at the age of four, she began studying ballet. Now a grand sujet with the prestigious Dutch National Ballet in Amsterdam, Michaela is also coauthor of *Taking Flight* and *Ballerina Dreams*. As the ambassador for War Child Netherlands, she advocates for the rights of women and child victims of war.

Tyler Feder is an illustrator, comedy writer, and ball of anxiety with bangs. She has illustrated for Netflix, Comedy Central, and ESPN, and her art has been featured by *Glamour* magazine, *Brigitte* magazine, and Mindy Kaling's instagram (twice!). Tyler lives in Chicago, Illinois, with her unhelpful assistant, Mitzvah (he is a cat).

Brenna Clarke Gray has a PhD in Canadian literature and teaches undergraduates about books and comics and writing and fandom and feminism at a community college in Vancouver, British Columbia, Canada. You can read her writing online at Book Riot and Graphixia, and you can find her on Twitter at @brennacgray.

Michelle Hiraishi is an illustrator living in Southern California. She enjoys illustrating images with strong story elements, and her mediums of choice are watercolors and ink. In her off-time, she loves to watch movies and reality TV shows, go café sketching, and venture out on road trips.

Mikki Kendall, a writer and occasional feminist, divides her time between two careers, a family, and brunch. Her writing covers a wide variety of topics, including media representation, police brutality, food insecurity, and other issues that impact marginalized people. Her nonfiction work has appeared in the *Guardian*, *Washington Post*, *Ebony*, *Essence*, *Time*, *Islamic Monthly*, and a host of other publications. She also commits acts of fiction largely focusing on black people in every situation under the sun, and a few under undefined celestial bodies. She can be found at mikkikendall. com and on Twitter @karnythia.

Kody Keplinger is the New York Times best-selling author of *The DUFF* (Designated Ugly Fat Friend) as well as several other books for kids and teens. She's a cofounder of Disability in Kidlit and a writing teacher in New York City.

Pomona Lake (she/her) is a graphic designer and visual artist who surreptitiously draws people on buses, keeps spreadsheets like other people keep a diary, makes casual misogynists ragequit on the daily, and secretly thinks that she can change the world with design. You can see more of her work at pomonalake.ca.

Malinda Lo is the author of the young adult novels *Ash*, *Huntress*, *Adaptation*, and *Inheritance*. Her novels have been finalists for the William C. Morris YA Debut Award, the Andre Norton Award, the Mythopoeic Fantasy Award, and the Lambda Literary Awards. Her nonfiction has been published by the New York Times Book Review, NPR, the *Huffington Post*, The Toast, the *Horn Book*, and AfterEllen. She lives in Massachusetts with her partner, and her website is malindalo.com.

Jessica Luther is an independent writer and investigative journalist whose work has appeared in the *Texas Observer*, and at *Sports Illustrated*, *Texas Monthly*, the *Guardian*, the *Atlantic*, and *Vice Sports*. Her book is titled *Unsportsmanlike Conduct: College Football and the Politics of Rape*.

Angie Manfredi is a youth services librarian in New Mexico. Working with kids and books is her greatest passion. She also loves film, deep-couch sitting, and trying to smash the white cishetero patriarchy.

Sarah McCarry (therejectionist.com/@therejectionist) is the author of the novels *All Our Pretty Songs*, *Dirty Wings*, and *About a Girl*, and the editor and publisher of the chapbook series Guillotine. Her books have been nominated for the Norton Award, been a finalist for the Lambda Literary Awards, and shortlisted for the Tiptree Award, and she is the recipient of a fellowship from the MacDowell Colony. She has written for the New York Times Book Review, *Glamour*, Book Riot, Tor.com, and others.

Kaye Mirza is a twenty-something Muslim blogger, essayist, and YA author. She is best known for creating the 2014 hashtag #YesAllWomen. Her writing has been featured on sites such as The Toast, School Library Journal's Teen Librarian Toolbox, and Love, InshAllah. Besides being an active advocate for diversity and intersectional feminism, she is currently a university junior pursuing an English major.

Lily Myers is a writer and spoken word artist from Seattle, Washington. She promotes feminism, self-love, and body positivity on her blog, *The Shapes We Make* (shapes wemake.com). Her debut novel, a coming-of-age story about family and body image, is due out from Philomel in 2017. Follow her on Twitter @lmyerspoetry.

Based in San Francisco, **Matt Nathanson** has evolved into one of the most applauded songwriters and engaging performers on the music scene today. His 2007 album, *Some Mad Hope*, yielded his breakthrough multi-platinum hit "Come on Get Higher." His 2013 release, *Last of the Great Pretenders*, debuted at #16 on the Billboard Top 200 while hitting #1 on iTunes' Alternative Albums chart. Nathanson's latest album, *Show Me Your Fangs*, is being hailed as his most adventurous and prolific album to date featuring the songs, "Giants," "Bill Murray," and "Adrenaline." Nathanson has been featured as a VH1 "You Oughta Know" artist, and has performed on *The Late Show with David Letterman*, *The Howard Stern Show*, *Ellen*, *Conan*, *The Tonight Show with Jay Leno*, *Jimmy Kimmel Live!*, *Dancing with the Stars*, *Rachael Ray*, and *The CMA Awards*, to name a few.

Alida Nugent is the author of *Don't Worry, It Gets Worse*, and *You Don't Have to Like Me*, available wherever books are sold. She lives in Brooklyn, where she gets lipstick on all her bagels, and writes at The-Frenemy.com.

Daniel José Older is the author of the young adult novel *Shadowshaper* (Scholastic, 2015), a New York Times Notable Book of 2015, which was shortlisted for the Kirkus Prize in Young Readers' Literature and the Andre Norton Award, and named one of Esquire's 80 Books Every Person Should Read. He also writes the Bone Street Rumba urban fantasy series. You can explore his thoughts on writing, read dispatches from his decade-long career as an NYC paramedic, hear his music at danieljoseolder.net, and find him on Twitter at @djolder.

Ashley Hope Pérez is the author of three novels. Her most recent, *Out of Darkness*, won a 2016 Printz honor and the 2016 Tomás Rivera Book Award. The New York Times Book Review described it as a "layered tale of color lines, love and struggle" in which "a tragedy, real and racial, swallows us whole." Pérez is an assistant professor of world literatures at Ohio State University.

Liz Prince is an autobiographical cartoonist whose first graphic memoir, *Tomboy*, was a 2015 Amelia Bloomer Project pick for books that promote feminism to younger readers. She can be found online at lizprincepower.com.

Rafe Posey's short story collection, *The Book of Broken Hymns*, was a Lambda Literary Awards finalist for Transgender Fiction. In earlier versions of himself, Rafe has been a bookseller, a seventh grade science teacher, a high school English teacher, and a film festival volunteer. At the moment, he teaches college composition in Baltimore.

Risa Rodil is a designer, illustrator, letterer, and a pop culture geek. Her body of work ranges from retro illustrations to brightly colored typography. She likes taking on new adventures to keep her enthusiasm going.

Becca Sexton and **Allison Peyton Steger**, the team behind the podcast This Week in Ladies (thisweekinladies.com), are a couple of punk-ass book jockeys living in Austin, Texas. They spend their time eating queso, haunting their local comic book shop, and getting way too invested in pub trivia.

Nova Ren Suma is the author of four novels, including the YA novels *Imaginary Girls*, *17 & Gone*, and #1 New York Times best seller *The Walls Around Us*. She is from various small towns across the Hudson Valley and now lives in New York City. Visit her online at novaren.com.

Courtney Summers lives and writes in Canada. She is the author of several young adult novels including *Cracked Up to Be*, *This Is Not a Test*, and *All the Rage*. Find her online at courtneysummers.ca.

Jen Talley has inhabited multiple identities as a student, writer, librarian, and artist. Her work has been featured on Buzzfeed and the fashion blog *Go Fug Yourself*, and can be seen at jentalley.com. Like Batgirl, she is still a librarian by day.

Shveta Thakrar is a writer of South Asian–flavored fantasy, a social justice activist, and a part-time nagini. Her work has appeared or is forthcoming in Flash Fiction Online, Interfictions Online, Clockwork Phoenix 5, Mythic Delirium, Uncanny, Faerie, Strange Horizons, Kaleidoscope: Diverse YA Science Fiction and Fantasy Stories, and Steam-Powered 2: More Lesbian Steampunk Stories. When not spinning stories about spider silk and shadows, magic and marauders, and courageous girls illuminated by dancing rainbow flames, Shveta crafts, devours books, daydreams, draws, travels, bakes, and occasionally even plays her harp. Learn more at shvetathakrar.com, and follow her on Twitter at @ShvetaThakrar.

Anne Thériault is a Toronto-based writer, activist, and social agitator. She is the author of *My Heart Is an Autumn Garage*, a short memoir about depression. Her work can be found in the *Washington Post*, *Vice*, *Jezebel*, The Toast, and others. Her comments on feminism, social justice, and mental health have been featured on TVO's *The Agenda*, CBC, CTV, Global and e-Talk Daily. She's really good at making up funny nicknames for cats.

Siobhan Vivian is the internationally bestselling author of several young adult novels, including *The List* and *The Last Boy and Girl in the World*. She also teaches creative writing at the University of Pittsburgh. Find her at siobhanvivian.com.

Suzannah Weiss is a writer whose work has appeared in the *Washington Post*, the *Village Voice*, *Vice*, *Salon*, *Glamour*, *Cosmopolitan*, *Elle*, *Marie Claire*, *Seventeen*, *Bitch*, *Bust*, Paper Magazine, and more. She holds degrees in Gender and Sexuality Studies, Modern Culture and Media, and cognitive neuroscience, which she uses mainly to overanalyze trashy television and argue over semantics. You can read some of her work at suzannahweiss.com and follow her on Twitter at @suzannahweiss.

Kayla Whaley is a senior editor at Disability in Kidlit and a graduate of the Clarion Writers' Workshop. Her work has appeared at The Toast, The Establishment, and in Uncanny Magazine, among other venues. You can follow her on Twitter at @Punkin OnWheels or find her at kaylawhaley.com.

Erika T. Wurth's novel, *Crazy Horse's Girlfriend*, was published by Curbside Splendor. Her first collection of poetry, *Indian Trains*, was published by the University of New Mexico's West End Press, and her second, *A Thousand Horses out to Sea*, is forthcoming from Mongrel Press. A writer of both fiction and poetry, she teaches creative writing at Western Illinois University and has been a guest writer at the Institute of American Indian Arts. Her work has appeared or is forthcoming in numerous journals, such as *Boulevard*, *Drunken Boat*, and *South Dakota Review*. She is represented by Peter Steinberg. She is Apache/Chickasaw/Cherokee and was raised outside of Denver.

Wendy Xu is a Brooklyn-based illustrator and comics artist, known for her Tumblr blog, *Angry Girl Comics*. She is cocreator of and currently draws the webcomic *Mooncakes* (mooncakescomic.tumblr.com). Her work has been featured in *Shattered: The Asian American Comics Anthology* and as part of the New York Historical Society's Chinese in America exhibit.

Constance Augusta Zaber is a student and writer currently living in Western Massachusetts. Her work is based on her experiences as a bisexual white trans woman living with depression and a serious love of fresh baked bread. You can find her at constancezaber.com or @augustazaber on Twitter.

OPYRIGHTS